IMPERIAL
China

THE ART OF THE HORSE
IN CHINESE HISTORY

EXHIBITION CATALOG

馬

Published by
Kentucky Horse Park
4089 Iron Works Parkway
Lexington, Kentucky 40511
www.kyhorsepark.com
in conjunction with
Harmony House Publishers
P.O. Box 90
Prospect, Kentucky 40050
502.228.2010

Library of Congress 99-85930
ISBN 1-56469-071-7

IMPERIAL

THE ART OF THE HORSE
IN CHINESE HISTORY

EXHIBITION CATALOG

Executive editor:	Mr. Bill Cooke
Written information by:	Mr. Bill Cooke
	Dr. Bill Booth
	Ms. Lynn Reynolds
	Ms. Jenifer Raisor
	Mr. Hu Zhisheng
	Mr. Jiang Wenxiao
	Mrs. Hu Xiaoli
	Mr. Zhang Tong
	Mr. Shi Dangshe
Editing by:	Ms. Lynn Reynolds
	Ms. Jenifer Raisor
	Ms. Gina Gibson
	Ms. Beth Cooke
Text Authentication by:	Dr. Kristin Stapleton
Photography by:	Mrs. Gao Yuying
	Mr. Wang Baoping
	Mr. Qui Zhiyu
	Ms. M. S. Rezny
Illustrations by:	Mr. Hu Zhisheng
	Ms. Yvonne Todd
	Mr. Mat Planet
Catalog design by:	Mr. Mat Planet

馬

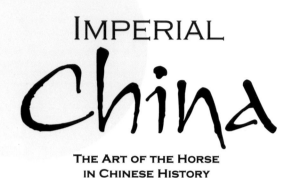

IMPERIAL
China

**THE ART OF THE HORSE
IN CHINESE HISTORY**

•

Exhibition Coordinators, USA:	Mr. John Nicholson, Mr. Bill Cooke
Exhibition Coordinators, China:	Mr. Li Bin, Mr. Zhang Tong
Guest Curator:	Dr. Bill R. Booth
Fund Raising Coordinator:	Mr. Roger Dalton
Exhibition Activities Coordinator:	Ms. Caroline Boone
Assistant Exhibition Activities Coordinator:	Ms. Julie Young
Gala Opening Reception Chairpersons:	Ms. Linda Green and Ms. Linda Morgan

The Kentucky Horse Park & International Museum of the Horse

Exhibition Design:	Ms. Gina Gibson
Exhibition Copy:	Mr. Bill Cooke and Ms. Jenifer Raisor
Exhibition Graphics Design:	Mr. Mat Planet
Shipping Coordinators:	Mr. Rob Hinkle and Ms. Jenifer Raisor
Exhibition Marketing:	Mr. Nore Ghibaudy
Volunteer Coordinator:	Ms. Georgina Beare
Educational Programs:	Ms. Barbara Dietrich, Ms. Pat Woodall, and Ms. Jane Martel
Security Director:	Captain Bob Pearl
Exhibition Accounting and Bookkeeping:	Mr. Michael Scales, Ms. Elizabeth Colliers, and Ms. Charlotte Lakers
Exhibition Area Construction:	Mr. Jamshid Baradaran, Mr. Jerry Columbia, Mr. Tony Holland, Mr. Steve Nickell, Mr. Donnie Powell, Mr. Spencer Holt, Mr. Tim Holt, Mr. David Jones, Mr. Todd Potter, Mr. Doug Robinson, Ms. Dana Pitcock
Additional Assistance:	Mr. Tim Jones and Ms. Pat Warren
Case Fabrication:	Fruland & Bowles, Inc., Toledo, Ohio
Track Lighting:	L. G. & E. Energy Corp., Kentucky Utilities Company
Track Lighting Design:	Kentucky Lighting Supply Company, Inc. (Eileen Rio)

馬

As for the horses, we have the shamans pray aloud in our presence before five pair of white horses who stand with heads turned toward the west, near the holy tree where twenty-seven paper offerings hang: "Oh Lord of Heaven, Oh Mongol leaders, Manchu princes, we pray to you for our swift horse. Through your power may their legs lift high, their manes toss; may they swallow the winds as they race, and grow ever sleeker as they drink in the mists, may they have fodder to eat, and be healthy and strong; may they have roots to nibble, and reach a great age. Guard them from ditches, front the precipices over Which my might fall; keep them far from thieves. Oh gods, guard them; Oh spirits, help them."

Qing Dynasty prayer, ca. AD 1680

Table of Contents

COMMONWEALTH OF KENTUCKY
OFFICE OF THE GOVERNOR

PAUL E. PATTON
GOVERNOR

700 CAPITOL AVENUE
SUITE 100
FRANKFORT, KY 40601
(502) 564-2611
FAX: (502) 564-2517

I am delighted to extend a warm welcome to all those attending the world exclusive exhibition, *Imperial China: The Art of the Horse in Chinese History.* Throughout my administration, I have stressed the importance of increasing educational opportunities for our citizens. Events such as this exhibition can only enhance our commitment to education. I am particularly proud that this outstanding exhibit, which ranks as one of the more significant international cultural events in Kentucky's history, is being held at one of our finest State facilities, The Kentucky Horse Park.

In an ever-shrinking world, it is important for us as Kentuckians and Americans to look beyond our borders in an attempt to gain insight and understanding of different cultures around the globe. Through increased knowledge comes the realization that those things we share in common are far greater than our differences. Over the past two decades, China's economic growth has astounded the world. Undoubtedly, as we move into the new millennium, they will have an ever-increasing effect on our daily lives. It is in the spirit of increasing our cultural understanding of the world's most populace nation that this exhibition came to be.

Both the people of Kentucky and of China have had a long and fascinating relationship with the horse. In the case of China, this relationship goes back over 5,000 years. How fitting then that this exhibition take place in Lexington, the city known as the "Horse Capital of the World," and at the Kentucky Horse Park, the world's premier equestrian learning and event facility.

After viewing the incredible assemblage of art and artifacts contained in this exhibition, it is my hope that you will take with you a new appreciation and understanding of one of the world's oldest civilizations. For those of you not native to our state, I would also invite you to take a few days to explore some of many other diverse attractions within our borders.

Sincerely,

Paul E. Patton

EDUCATION
PAYS

AN EQUAL OPPORTUNITY EMPLOYER M/F/D

KENTUCKY HORSE PARK

| PAUL E. PATTON
GOVERNOR | SECRETARY ANN LATTA
TOURISM DEVELOPMENT CABINET | WALT ROBERTSON
COMMISSION CHAIRMAN | JOHN NICHOLSON
EXECUTIVE DIRECTOR |

I am pleased to welcome you to the Kentucky Horse Park for the world exclusive presentation of *Imperial China: The Art of the Horse in Chinese History*. It is a large part of the mission of the Horse Park to celebrate mankind's long partnership with the horse. We believe that this exhibition is a unique and stimulating way to continue to fulfill that mission.

Now in its twenty-second year, the Kentucky Horse Park has evolved into one of the world's leading equestrian educational, entertainment and event facilities. The Park, which is dedicated to all breeds of horse, serves as a theme park for the horse industry and celebrates Kentucky's special relationship with this majestic animal. It is also the venue for over sixty annual horse shows and competitions in a number of different equestrian disciplines. The National Horse Center, which surrounds the main visitor parking lot, is the home to fourteen leading equine industry organizations and confirms this area's reputation as the "Horse Capital of the World."

It is our sincere hope that in addition to viewing the *Imperial China* exhibition, that you will visit the many attractions and events at the Park. I believe that you will find our staff most anxious to help make your visit to the Kentucky Horse Park an interesting, memorable and, most importantly, a fun experience.

John Nicholson
Executive Director
Kentucky Horse Park

4089 Iron Works Parkway, Lexington, Kentucky 40511   (606)233-4303(TDD)   FAX(606)254-0253   www.imh.org/khp

An Equal Opportunity Employer M/F/D

KENTUCKY HORSE PARK

PAUL E. PATTON	SECRETARY ANN LATTA	WALT ROBERTSON	JOHN NICHOLSON
GOVERNOR	TOURISM DEVELOPMENT CABINET	COMMISSION CHAIRMAN	EXECUTIVE DIRECTOR

On behalf of the Kentucky Horse Park Commission, I am proud to welcome you to Imperial China: The Art of the Horse in Chinese History. This world exclusive exhibition is the first ever to explore the role of the horse in more than 3,000 years of Chinese history and culture.

For many generations, Lexington, Kentucky has had a worldwide association with the horse. Since it opened in 1978, the Kentucky Horse Park has played a significant role in this community's international equine reputation. We hope you agree that it is entirely appropriate that a world class exhibition which explores the role of the horse in one of the oldest cultures on earth be held at this facility which is dedicated to mankind's eternal bond with the horse.

It is our sincere hope that you will find this exhibition fascinating and enjoyable. If this is your first visit to the Kentucky Horse Park, we hope that you will take the time to visit our horses and to experience the various attractions on the Park.

Please accept our sincere appreciation for your interest in this exhibition and for your support of the Kentucky Horse Park.

Walt Robertson
Chairman
Kentucky Horse Park Commission

K E N T U C K Y
TOURISM DEVELOPMENT CABINET

2400 CAPITAL PLAZA TOWER
500 MERO STREET
FRANKFORT, KENTUCKY 40601

Phone 502-564-4270
Fax 502-564-1512

PAUL E. PATTON, Governor
ANN R. LATTA, Secretary
DAVID LOVELACE, Deputy Secretary

It is with pleasure that I welcome you to the Kentucky Horse Park's exhibition, *Imperial China: The Art of the Horse in Chinese History.* This world exclusive exhibition is one of the largest and most spectacular to ever come out of China. It is our sincere hope that you will agree that it is a fascinating and stimulating exploration of one of the world's oldest and richest cultures.

After viewing the exhibition, I would like to encourage you to visit the many attractions of the Kentucky Horse Park. The Park is a one thousand acre facility dedicated to mankind's love of the horse and we are proud of its national reputation as an unequaled equestrian facility.

I would also like to suggest that you take the time to visit and explore some of the other wonderful regions and attractions of the Commonwealth. Our state has been blessed by a rich diversity and we would be most pleased to assist you in planning your personal Kentucky odyssey. Please give us a call at the Kentucky travel information line at 1-800-225-8747.

I hope your visit to the *Imperial China* exhibition and to the Kentucky Horse Park is a rewarding experience and that you will visit us again at the earliest possible time.

Ann R. Latta, Secretary
Kentucky Tourism Development Cabinet

EDUCATION PAYS

An Equal Opportunity Employer

Preface

China is a land of myths and mysteries shrouded in the mist of history. Throughout the course of Chinese history, one animal has exerted a tremendous influence over its development - the horse. In an attempt to define the horse's impact on the development of Chinese civilization and art, this exhibition was created.

China has a long and unbroken history which dates from at least 7000 BC. While their invention of writing is ascribed to the mythical Yellow Emperor, Huang Di in the 26th century BC, by the second century BC the Chinese were keeping very detailed records that were unrivaled in the western world until the eighteenth and nineteenth centuries. While ancient Greek, Egyptian, Babylonian, Assyrian, and Summerian civilizations were thought to be somewhat older than China's, more recent archaeological discoveries now suggest that an organized Chinese civilization was in place by as early as 9000 BC. The Shang dynasty was in full bloom while the great Pyramids of ancient Egypt were being completed. The Qin dynasty was coming to an end when the Roman Republic was at its height, and the Tang Dynasty was producing some of the richest art treasures seen in this exhibition during the medieval period of European history. The Ming dynasty was comparable in time to the Renaissance in Europe, and the last dynasty, the Qing, began before the American Revolution and ended shortly after the Wright brothers first flight ushering in the modern age of aviation.

The domesticated horse does not seem to have appeared in Chinese cultural history until sometime around 3000 BC. There is strong evidence that China contributed some of the world's most important equestrian inventions including the stirrup, the horse collar, and the first effective equine harnessing system. The harnessing system, the first that did not bear directly on the horse's windpipe, would remain superior to any system developed in the west for another 1,000 years.

The exquisite items contained within this collection are but a reflection of the grandeur of Chinese Imperial artifacts. From the terracotta warriors taken from the tomb of China's first emperor, Qin Shi Huang, to the hunting scenes painted in the Qing dynasty, the richness of Chinese culture and its art are shown in the objects selected for this exhibition.

Bill Cooke, Director of the International Museum of the Horse, initiated plans for this exhibition in December of 1996. He was encouraged to pursue this project by John Nicholson, the Executive Director of the Museum's parent organization, The Kentucky Horse Park, who has worked tirelessly to insure the exhibition's success. I was asked to serve as the Guest Curator, due in large measure to the work I had done on the study of Emperor Qin Shi Huang. This had led to a friendship and working relationship with Zhang Tong, Exhibitions Officer with the Administrative Bureau of Museums & Archaeological Data of Shaanxi Province, who was assigned to work with us to organize the exhibition. His friendship and professionalism resulted in a collaboration, the results of which are the remarkable examples of Chinese art and artifacts seen in this exhibition.

This exhibition would not have been possible without the efforts of Zhang Tong, and the support given to him by Li Bin, Director of Foreign Affairs Department and Director General Zhang Ting Hao of The Administrative Bureau of Museums & Archaeological Data of Shaanxi Province, The People's Republic of China. Numerous museums, archaeological research centers, and repositories of Chinese cultural treasures were opened to us, where we were given the opportunity to select rare pieces of equestrian art and items commonly used by the nobility. Many of these pieces have never been exhibited, even in China.

Any exhibition of this size, importance and complexity requires the efforts of many people within the staff of the museum, state and local government, fundraisers and volunteers from the community. To each and every individual whose ideas, industry, time and effort were given to this project, I extend my most sincere thanks and appreciation for the tireless work which has culminated in this exhibition.

PREFACE

This is a world exclusive exhibition, and one of the largest ever to leave China, featuring more than 350 artifacts and spanning more than 3,000 years. It is appropriate that this exhibition, featuring artifacts and art objects relating to the horse be shown at the world's largest museum dedicated to the impact of the horse on human history, International Museum of the Horse at the Kentucky Horse Park.

My hope is that as you view this collection you will consider the importance and historic significance of these objects in their relationship to life in China from the Zhou Dynasty (ca. 1100 BC) to the present century. As you leave this exhibit consider how your expanded understanding of Chinese culture has given you a new and better perspective of the Chinese, their history, and culture.

Dr. Bill R. Booth, Guest Curator
Professor Emeritus of Art History
Morehead State University
Morehead, Kentucky

Acknowledgements

The staging of an exhibition of this size and scope would be impossible without the cooperation and collaboration of innumerable people in both the Commonwealth of Kentucky and in the People's Republic of China. I am particularly grateful for the encouragement and assistance received from Governor Paul Patton, Secretary of the Governor's Cabinet, Crit Luallen, Tourism Cabinet Secretary, Ann Latta, Lexington Mayor Pam Miller, David Lord and his Lexington Convention and Visitors' Bureau staff, and unwavering support of the Kentucky Horse Park Commission, the Advisory Board of the International Museum of the Horse, and the Kentucky Horse Park Foundation and their respective chairpersons, Mr. Walt Robertson, Dr. Donald Jacobs, and Ms. Nina Bonnie.

In the People's Republic of China, I am grateful to all of our colleagues at the Administrative Bureau of Museums and Archaeological Data of Shaanxi Province, and to numerous museum officials throughout Shaanxi Province, for making the organization of this exhibition such a wonderful and enlightening experience. I would like to thank the Bureau's Director General, Mr. Zhang Ting Hao, for his steadfast cooperation and enthusiasm for this project. Special thanks goes to the two people with whom we have worked most closely, Director of the Foreign Affairs Department, Mr. Li Bin and our Exhibition Officer, Mr. Zhang Tong. These individuals have not only gone above and beyond in their efforts to make this exhibition successful, they have also shown to me and our staff an unprecedented level of hospitality and friendship during our visits to Xi'an.

Also worthy of special note are the members of our Exhibition Steering Committee and its co-chairpersons, Caroline Boone and Roger Dalton. Without their countless hours coordinating our fund raising efforts, and organizing all exhibit-related events and activities, this exhibition would not have been possible. I would also like to give special recognition to our regional fund raising coordinators, Wayne Martin, Rick Anderson, William T. Robinson, III, and David Anderson, and to our Guest Curator, Dr. Bill Booth whose many previous visits to China opened so many doors for us. His knowledge, experience, and guidance have been invaluable.

Closer to home, my co-workers at the Kentucky Horse Park have shown yet again a degree of professionalism, resourcefulness, and pride that defies belief. Their efforts in dealing with the myriad of issues necessary to stage an event of this magnitude, in addition to their many other duties, have been exceptional. Of particular note is the Park's maintenance and construction staff. The skills and creativity they have demonstrated in the construction of the additional gallery space necessary to house Imperial China, with minimal outside assistance, not only produced an exceptional special exhibition complex, but also saved the Park hundreds of thousands of dollars.

To my Museum staff, who for more than two years have put up with my "China obsession," and have pitched in to assure that regular museum operations have continued, goes my deepest appreciation. The additional burdens that all of these dedicated professionals have born in both the preparation of the exhibition facilities and in the production of the exhibition itself, have been truly inspirational. To Gina Gibson, Mat Planet, Jenifer Raisor, Lynn Reynolds, and Pat Woodall, thank you.

And last, but certainly not least, I offer my sincere thanks to my boss, Kentucky Horse Park Executive Director, John Nicholson. Were it not for his incredible vision, leadership, and tireless efforts, this exhibition would still be but a dream. Through good times and bad, his unflagging faith, friendship, and support of the Imperial China exhibition have meant more to me than he will ever know.

Bill Cooke, Director
International Museum of the Horse
Kentucky Horse Park

Sponsors to the Exhibition

Patrons
Commonwealth of Kentucky
Lexington Convention and Visitors Bureau
Gray Communications, Inc.
The Kentucky Horse Park Foundation
The James S. and James L. Knight Foundation / The Lexington Herald-Leader

Sponsors
National City Bank
The Robert J. Kleberg, Jr. & Helen C. Kleberg Foundation
Louisville Gas & Electric Corp.
    Kentucky Utilities Company
    Louisville Gas & Electric Company
    West Kentucky Energy
Delta Air Lines
Ashland, Inc. & Valvoline, Inc.
Greenbaum, Doll & McDonald PLLC
Host Communications, Inc
Keeneland Association, Inc.
Kentucky Thoroughbred Association
Lexington-Fayette Urban County Government
Dr. & Mrs. Donald Jacobs
Mr. Robert B. Morgan
Mr. & Mrs. John Schiff, Jr.

Contributors
Ms. Caroline Boone
Stites and Harbison
Ms. Helen Alexander
Mr. Louis Carmichael
Ms. Helen B. Chenery
The R. C. Durr Foundation
The William Stamps Farrish Foundation
Fasig-Tipton Company, Inc.
Mr. Gerald Healy
Mrs. Eugenie and Joseph Jones Family Foundation
The Junior League of Lexington
Mrs. W. Paul Little
Mr. & Mrs. John R. Donna Hall
Maker's Mark
Ms. Marcie A. Newman
Duncan Machinery
The Rosenthal Foundation
Stoll, Kennon & Park LLP

Lenders to the Exhibition

The vast majority of the art and artifacts contained in this exhibition were generously provided from museums and institutions throughout Shaanxi Province, The Peoples' Republic of China.

Chinese Institutions

The Shaanxi Archaeological Research Institute
Museum of Baoji City
Shaanxi Baoji Provincial Archaeological Research Center
Shaanxi Xi'an Beilin Museum; Shaanxi County Museum
Shaanxi Fengxiang County Museum
Shaanxi Fupeng County Museum
Shaanxi History Museum
Shaanxi Longxian County Museum
Maoling Museum
Shaanxi Municipal Relics Protection and Archaeological Research Center
Shaanxi Mizhi County Relics Administration
Shaanxi Municipal Archaeological Team
Museum of the Qin Shi Huang Terracotta Army
Xi'an Institute of Cultural Relics and Archaeology
Xianyang Museum
Shaanxi Zhaoling Museum
Shaanxi Provincial Zhouyuan Museum.

Other Lenders

The Governor's Mansion, Commonwealth of Kentucky
Dr. Bill R. Booth

	周	Zhou	"joe"
	秦	Qin	"chin"
	汉	Han	"hahn"
	隋	Sui	"sway"
	唐	Tang	"tahng"
	宋	Song	"sung"
	元	Yuan	"yuwahn"
	明	Ming	"meeng"
	清	Qing	"cheeng"

Romanization.   Chinese is transcribed here using the Pinyin system of romanization adopted by the People's Republic of China and now in general use.

Names.   Chinese names are shown in traditional fashion with the given name following the surname.

The following Pinyin consonants sometimes present problems in pronunciation.

Romanized Pinyin Letter	Approximate sound in English
c	aunt**s**
q	**ch**ase
x	**sh**e
zh	ur**ge**

Pronunciation Guide to Chinese Dynasties

Romanized Pinyin Spelling	Approximate sound in English
Shang	shahng
Zhou	joe
Qin	chin
Han	hahn
Sui	sway
Tang	tahng
Song	sung
Yuan	yuwahn
Ming	meeng
Qing	cheeng

TIMELINE

CHINESE HISTORY & CULTURE

• **Zhou Dynasty**
ca. 1100-256 BC

• Western Zhou
ca. 1100-771 BC

• Eastern Zhou
770-256 BC

• Spring & Autumn Period
770-476 BC

• Warring States Period
475-221 BC

• **Han Dynasty**
206 BC - AD 220

• Western Han
206 BC - AD 8

Xin (Wang Mang usurpation AD 9-23)

• Eastern Han
AD 25-220

• **Qin Dynasty**
221-207 BC

• **Western Jin D**
256-316

• Eastern J
317-420

• Three Kingdon
220-280

• Reign of First Emperor, Qin Shi Huang
246-210 BC

• Great Wall begun
215 BC

• Great Wall completed
AD 214

• Chinese invent paper
ca. AD 100

• Silk Road opened
139 BC

• Birth of Buddha
563 BC

• Buddhism enters China from India
ca. AD 150

• Birth of Confucius
551 BC

• Development of Breast Strap Harness in China
ca. 250 BC

• Chinese invent stirrup
AD 322

THE WORLD

• Reign of King Solomon
961-922 BC

• Crucifixion of Jesus Christ
AD 33

Reign of
Attilla the Hun
AD 433-453

• First Olympic games
776 BC

• Hannibal crosses Alps
218 BC

• Founding of Rome
753 BC

• Parthenon Built
447-432 BC

Constantinople becomes •
capital of Roman Empire
AD 330

• Tang Dynasty
618-907

• Song Dynasty
960-1279

• Ming Dynasty
1368-1644

• Qing Dynasty
1644-1911

sty

nasty

• Sui Dynasty
589-618

• Northern Song
960-1127

Southern Song
1127-1279

hern and Northern Dynasties

nasty

• Yuan Dynasty
1279-1368

• Five Dynasties
907-960

• Polo comes to China from Persia
ca. 700

• Genghis Khan founds Mongol Empire
1206

• Earliest dated woodblock print
Diamond Sutra
868

• Marco Polo's journey to China
1271-1292

Two-year-old Puyi •
named China's last emperor
1908

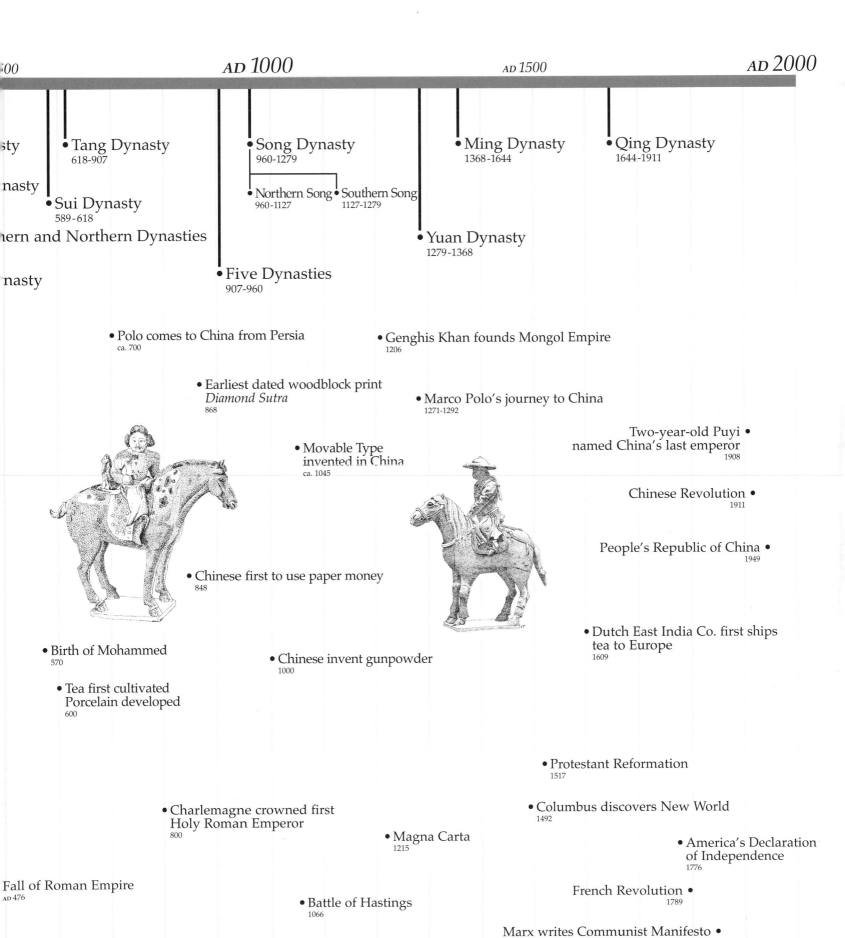

• Movable Type
invented in China
ca. 1045

Chinese Revolution •
1911

People's Republic of China •
1949

• Chinese first to use paper money
848

• Dutch East India Co. first ships
tea to Europe
1609

• Birth of Mohammed
570

• Chinese invent gunpowder
1000

• Tea first cultivated
Porcelain developed
600

• Protestant Reformation
1517

• Charlemagne crowned first
Holy Roman Emperor
800

• Columbus discovers New World
1492

• Magna Carta
1215

• America's Declaration
of Independence
1776

Fall of Roman Empire
AD 476

French Revolution •
1789

• Battle of Hastings
1066

Marx writes Communist Manifesto •
1848

The Horse in Chinese History

Bill Cooke

The Horse in Chinese History

Bill Cooke

Introduction

Throughout China's long and storied past, no animal has impacted its history as greatly as the horse. From its domestication in northeastern China around 5,000 years ago, the horse has been an integral figure in the creation and survival of the Middle Kingdom. Its significance was such that as early as the Shang dynasty (ca. 1600-1100 BC), horses and the vehicles they powered were entombed with their owners so as to be with them in the next life. During the Western Zhou dynasty (ca. 1100-771 BC), military might was measured by the number of war chariots available to a particular kingdom. As the empire grew, horses became essential for maintaining contact and control and for transporting goods and supplies throughout the vast and diverse country.

Sun Ji, one of the leading authorities regarding the history of the horse in China, stated that there were three major periods of significant change in China's equine population. The first was during the Han dynasty (206 BC-AD 220) when, under Emperor Wudi, the Chinese expended vast amounts of resources in an effort to import superior horses from the West. The second occurred during the Tang dynasty (618-907) when horses were improved both by advances in domestic breeding practices and through the importation of Arab-type and Turkish horses. Finally, during the Yuan dynasty (1279-1368) there was an overall decline in horse quality with the deterioration of the remnants of the Tang breeding programs. Ironically, this decline occurred during the first imperial dynasty controlled by nomadic horsemen.

China's very survival relied on its equestrian prowess. From the fourth century BC forward, the empire's greatest threat came from its nomadic neighbors to the north and west. By the rise of the Han dynasty, the Chinese had reluctantly been forced to abandon the war chariot in favor of mounted cavalry in order to face this threat. From the Xiongnu to the Mongols and Manchus, these northern tribes fielded some of the finest cavalry the world would ever see, while providing a constant thorn in the side of the Chinese.

The Chinese quest to maintain adequate equestrian forces to combat the nomadic raiders became a common thread throughout the imperial period. Massive military campaigns were waged in search of superior "blood-sweating horses" from the Ferghana (Dayuan) far to the west. These sojourns, while tremendously expensive in terms of resources and manpower, not only helped to improve the quality of Chinese horses, but also led to the establishment of major contacts between East and West and the opening of the famous Silk Roads.

The horse also played an important role in the mythology of early China. Closely associated with the dragon, both were thought capable of flight and of carrying their riders to the "home of the immortals." The ability to fly has been associated with survival throughout all of Chinese history.

Chinese genius produced three of the most significant inventions in equestrian history: an effective harnessing system based on the breast-strap, the stirrup, and the horse collar. Their harnessing system was the first to effectively utilize the horse's power without hampering its ability to breathe. It allowed for the development of shafted horse-drawn vehicles far more advanced and efficient than those of their counterparts in the West. In fact, it would be more than a millennium before the breast-strap harnessing system would arrive in Europe. The invention of the stirrup was equally important and meant that for the first time mounted cavalry had a secure platform from which to fight. Sun Ji ranks the invention of the breast strap harnessing system and the stirrup, along with the invention of paper and gunpowder, as the four most significant Chinese inventions in their impact on world history.[1]

As the military significance of the horse increased, so too did its role in leisure and recreational activities. "Dancing" dressage horses delighted emperors in court ceremonies as early as the Han dynasty, and reached their zenith with the elaborate performances of the Tang dynasty. Also during the Tang, both polo and hunting from horseback became fashionable for members of both sexes.

One of the great paradoxes of Chinese history is that despite the horse's significance to the survival of the empire, domestic horse breeding programs were rarely successful. As a result, China was forced to spend vast sums to purchase horses from its nomadic neighbors throughout most all of the imperial period. The Tang (618-907) - the first dynasty in China to be initiated by a people with a strong equestrian heritage - did make strong attempts to increase both the quantity and the quality of their horses. They established an intricate structure for managing their herds and enacted strict laws governing the treatment of the royal steeds. However, during the waning years of the Tang dynasty, their horse management system had fallen into disarray.

In many ways the Song dynasty (960-1279) represented a cultural highpoint in Chinese history. The Song, however, lacking the equestrian and militaristic traditions of the Tang, faced serious horse shortages throughout their reign.

Throughout much of the imperial period, China's salvation rested with the inability of the nomadic tribes to unite into an effective fighting force. That changed, however, in 1211 when the great general Genghis Khan turned his Mongol horsemen toward China. These were some of the finest cavalry forces the world had ever seen. It was said that, "...the Mongol horsemen could travel up to ten days, subsisting only on horse's blood, which they drank from a pierced vein."[2] Although Genghis would not live to see the results of the campaign, in 1279 the Yuan dynasty was established under the control of his grandson, Khubilai Khan.

By the beginning of the Ming dynasty (1368-1644) the horse's significance in transportation had been somewhat diminished by further development in water-based shipping. The horse did, however, remain essential for military security, but was in short supply. Towards the end of the Ming dynasty the Manchus became a significant force to be dealt with by the Chinese. They had refused to leave Beijing after being invited to help quell a rebellion in 1644. That same year they established the Qing dynasty (1644-1911). Based in no small part on their equestrian skills, the Qing established one of the greatest empires in China's long history

While the horse may have diminished in practical importance in modern China, the spirit of Equus still runs deeply throughout Chinese art and culture. This is not to say that horses do not constitute a significant presence in China today. In 1995, it was estimated that the horse population of China exceeded 11,000,000. This equates to one-sixth of the horses in the world and includes more than 26 distinct breeds.[3]

The Horse in Early China
First Domestication

The first domestication of the horse is thought to have taken place around 6,000 years ago somewhere on the Eurasian steppe. Comparisons with cultures in other parts of the world suggest that the horse probably first served as a source of meat, milk and hides. While it has long been accepted that humans harnessed horses prior to riding them, new archaeological research in Eurasia now appears to push the date for the first horseback riding back to approximately 4000 BC. David Anthony's recent study of the excavations from Dereivka in the Ukrainian steppes have unearthed horse teeth from this period which show distinct signs of bit wear. This would indicate that man became mounted shortly after domestication - some 3,000 years prior to significant horseback riding in the Western world.[4] In China, domestication occurred at approximately 3000 BC.

Because of the vast influence of the pastoral cultures that surrounded China to the north and west, any study of the horse in China also requires a look at the equestrian developments there. According to Franz Hancar, the selective breeding of horses began in Western Asia during the first millennium BC. More specifically, this was the large area north of Iran, including the modern day countries of Kazakhstan, Turkmenistan, Uzbekistan, Tadzhikistan, and Kirghizistan that Hancar refers to as "Turan."

Possibly the best-preserved evidence of the early Eurasian horse can be found at the fifth century BC Scythian site in the Altai Mountains. Here, at the Pazyryk kurgans (grave mounds), sixty-nine complete horses and eighteen partial skeletons were discovered frozen in ice. The horses can be divided into two distinct groups. The smaller of the two stand approximately 12.2 hands, slightly shorter than the wild Przewalski horse. The larger of the group, however, measures 14.3 hands, taller than a modern Arabian horse. Hancar has hypothesized that the larger and more refined of these horses exhibit the result of extensive selective breeding, and are, in fact, early Turan horses.

A. P. Okladnikov observed that the Pazyryk horses "were excellent riding horses of the best breeds of the East, of noble blood, stately and lively jumpers of gold-brown color. They were not fed green fodder but selected grain, and were kept in well-attended stalls."[5] This would certainly indicate that by this period the increased size seen in the Pazyryk horses resulted not only from a rudimentary system of selective breeding in place, but also from better care and nutrition.

China's first horse stock may well have been based on a domesticatable variant of the wild Przewalski horse. These may have been crossed with some imported stock, and were undoubtedly improved by primitive selective breeding. Matched teams, distinguished both as to color and to size, were available in the stables of the Shang kings as early as the fourteenth century BC. By the tenth century BC, these horses had evolved to resemble the present day Mongol pony. Poems and documents dating from early in the first millennium BC refer frequently to prized horses of special colors and characteristics. The judging of horses was recognized early as a special art.

Early on, the Chinese seemed aware that the best horses came from the north and the west.

> In 538 BC the ruler of a northern Chinese state boasted that it feared no enemy
> because, among other assets, it had many horses. But one of his ministers rebuked
> his complacency and asserted that horses, apparently meaning the best horses,
> came from "northern Chi." The exact location of this area is debated, but it was
> approximately in the northern tip of the modern Shanxi Province, then a border
> area inhabited by nomads who may have been partly sinicized. In connection with

the fierce struggles between the contending Chinese states in the fourth century BC, emphasis was laid upon the strategic importance of controlling the horses of this region and importing horses from the northern nomads known as Hu. In the third century BC, the philosopher Hsün-tzu [Xunzi] named fast horses as the special product of the "north sea," that is, of the vaguely defined region north of China.[6]

The First Horse-Drawn Vehicles

The horse-drawn chariot was developed shortly after domestication in the Fertile Crescent around 4000 BC - 3,700 years earlier than its appearance in China. The chariot did not develop independently in ancient China, but was adopted from the non-Chinese tribes to the north, who had themselves acquired it from tribes living farther west in Central Asia and beyond.

The horse and chariot burials at the funeral site of King Wuding (r. ca. 1200 - 1118 BC) of the Shang dynasty at Anyang, mark the first archaeological evidence of the horse's use in wheeled transport in China, dating from the late thirteenth century BC. Some scholars, however, now feel that the chariot's arrival could have been as much as four centuries earlier. Prior to the appearance of the chariot in China, transportation was limited to rivers and canals connected by footpaths.

The Anyang chariots are very similar to others discovered in the Caucasus region between the Black and Caspian Seas. Both examples share a low open-fronted box or driver's platform, many spoked wheels, and felloes (wheel rims) composed of two pieces of bent wood. The fact that weapons were regularly found in conjunction with these sites indicates that these vehicles were already being utilized for their military potential.

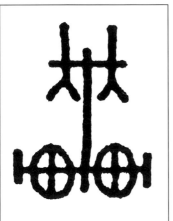

Figure 1

Excavations show that the horses used to power the early chariots stood between 13.3 and 14.3 hands and had heavy heads and stocky bones similar to the modern Przewalski horse. (One hand equals four inches. Horses are measured by calculating the distance from the ground to the top of the withers - the high point on the back of the horse located at the base of the neck.) Early pictographs for chariots (Fig. 1) indicate that the Shang drove two horses in a team arranged around a central pole. The presence of the central pole and yoke would imply the use of the inefficient throat-and-girth type harness, which will be discussed later.

The early chariots of the Shang dynasty were made of wood, with only parts such as the ends of the axle and the end of the central pole covered with bronze caps both for protection and decorative purposes. The chariots were made up of a central pole with the axle at the end, forming a cross on which the chariot body was placed. The body was usually rectangular, with railings on four sides and a door in the rear. The axle of the chariot protruded out of the wheels on both sides. On the front part of the pole was a crossbar on which were tied the yokes.

Some have speculated that the chariot was first brought to China through armed conflict with its nomadic neighbors. This, however, would seem unlikely given the vast amount of technology and infrastructure that would have been necessary to take full advantage of the chariot's potential. The chariot would have been of little use without specialists accomplished in the arts of horse training, veterinary medicine, driving, harness design and production, wheel construction, etc.

An affable exchange with one of Shang's northern neighbors would seem to be a more likely scenario. It is known that Shang King Wuding's consort, Fu Hao, came from one of the tribes to the north. One could speculate that possibly the technology and technicians necessary to effectively utilize the chariot might have been brought to the Shang court as part of her dowry. This could also help explain the number of northern artifacts found at Wuding's burial site at Anyang.

The actual use of the chariot and its military effectiveness are topics still hotly debated. Excavations have shown that the two-horse chariot of the Shang and subsequent four-horse chariot of the Western Zhou dynasty (ca. 1100-771 BC) would have been heavy and hard to maneuver due to their centrally placed axle. It is hard to imagine that these would have been effective fighting machines. It also should be noted that throughout the world, wherever the chariot appeared, its military effectiveness was limited to relatively flat and smooth terrain.

A description appearing in the *Sunzi Bingfa* (Sunzi's *Art of War*) suggests that the chariot was used more as a mobile command post around which military units were structured rather than as an actual fighting machine.

> One chariot carries three mailed officers, seventy-two foot troops accompany it.
> Additionally, there are ten cooks and servants, five men to take care of uniforms,
> five grooms in charge of fodder, and five men to collect firewood and draw water.
> Seventy-five men to one light chariot, twenty-five to one baggage wagon, so that
> taking the two together one hundred men compose a company.[7]

Figure 2

The Zhou chariots also appear to have been elaborately decorated. In the "Book of Odes" (*Shijing*), chariots (Fig. 2) were described as displaying brilliantly colored banners with oxtail tassels and harness bells. The amount and the impracticality of the ornamentation reinforce the hypothesis that the chariot was principally a ceremonial vehicle or mobile command post.

Regardless of their usage, by the middle of the eighth century BC, the measure of a state's importance was ascertained by the number of war chariots and horses it possessed. The chariot's association with wealth and power no doubt led to the high esteem in which they were held. With the rise of the Zhou, the use of chariots also spread beyond the royal household. As a result, throughout the Zhou dynasty, horse and chariot burials become associated more often with unidentified tombs.

Zhou chariots evolved to include much more bronze ornamentation than those of the Shang. The box, or driver's compartment, had straight, decorative bands decorating its sides. Bronze parts were also used as components of the axle and the harness. The most important and decorative section of the axle was a round pole-holder near the box of the chariot. Axle caps were held in place by bronze linchpins.

In the fourth century BC poem *The Great Summons*, Qu Yuan, in exile for nine years, reflects on the ornate vehicles of the royal court.

> And round the house a covered way should run
> Where horses might be trained.
> And sometimes riding, sometimes going afoot
> You shall explore, O Soul, the parks of spring;
> Your jeweled axles gleaming in the sun
> And yoke inlaid with gold;
> Or amid orchids and sandal-trees
> Shall walk in the Dark woods.
> O Soul come back and live for these delights![8]

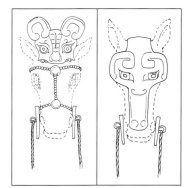

Figure 3   *Figure 4*

Not only were the Zhou chariots elaborately decorated, so too was their harness. The harness included a center frontlet and bronze ornaments forming a mask on the eyes and nose of the horse (Fig. 3 & 4). A second mask was often mounted above the ears. The harness straps were decorated with beads, cowry shells, or bronze plaques, and passed through decorated cross-tubes which, by the Qin dynasty (221-207 BC), were sometimes crafted of gold and silver.

From the late Shang dynasty, bits generally had rectangular cheek pieces, and by the end of the Western Zhou period the cheek pieces were decorated with elaborate designs, particularly of coiled dragons.

Qin Dynasty Vehicles at the Mausoleum of China's First Emperor

One of the most remarkable discoveries in the history of archaeology occurred in 1974 when two farmers digging a well discovered the mausoleum of China's first emperor, Qin Shi Huang (r. 221 - 210 BC). In addition to more than 7,000 life-size terra-cotta soldiers, the site contains over 500 chariot horses, 116 cavalry horses and 130 battle chariots. All of the horses stand approximately 13.2 hands.

In 1980, our knowledge of Qin vehicles was greatly enhanced with the discovery of a spectacular bronze chariot and a bronze carriage. Crafted at one-half life-size scale, each vehicle was fully harnessed to four horses. The harness was also constructed of bronze. While both vehicles were severely damaged, an exhaustive restoration resulted in the first examples of the harnessing and vehicle construction techniques used during the Qin dynasty.

The two bronze carriages discovered in the First Emperor's tomb were obviously superior vehicles of the nobility. The first carriage was a *li-che*. A prominent feature of this carriage is the canopy. The second carriage found in the tomb was an *an-che* (small carriage with seats) [Fig. 5]. Such carriages were first made during the Zhou dynasty and were for the use of kings, dukes, feudal lords, queens, consorts, and venerated elders. The size of a carriage and the number of horses used varied according to the rank, status, and sex of the occupant. All *an che* had to have a cover and a canopy. There were steps on three sides of the carriage, and handrails in front and on the two sides. The floor of the carriage was covered with a soft mattress. The body of the carriage was 88 cm high, and long enough for the occupant to ride lying down. The driver's seat was outside, a major change from earlier carriages, in which the driver sat together with his master.

Figure 5

There are dragon designs all over the carriages. The Kui-dragon on the carriages is a stylized design resembling clouds. The hollow bricks found at the site of Xianyang Palace also had images of dragons, depicting them clasping pearls in their claws. The emperor compared himself to the dragon and his empress to a phoenix, a legendary bird said to be auspicious. This tradition of using the dragon and phoenix as symbols of imperial power continued through all subsequent …dynasties.

The bronze horses and carriages unearthed at the First Emperor's mausoleum were made of an alloy of copper, tin, and lead, with traces of some ten other metallic and nonmetallic elements including iron, aluminum, silicon, titanium, and calcium.[9]

The Demise of the Chariot in Warfare

By the latter portion of the Eastern Zhou dynasty (770-256 BC), chariots had greatly decreased in value as prestige items, being replaced by intricately decorated individual weapons. With the increasing strength of the Xiongnu along the northern border and the rise in the importance of cavalry, the role of the chariots decreased significantly. The varied terrain over which battles were fought also made chariots less valuable. The death knell for the chariot probably came during the Qin conflict with the southern states of Chu and Yue. The terrain in these areas was either mountainous or flooded - totally unsuited for chariot warfare.

The Carriages of the Rich in Chang'an

Chariots still maintained an important role in the transportation of government officials during the Han dynasty. Possibly because of the chronic shortage of horses, anyone other than officials and a few of the rich were banned from using carriages and chariots. In an account written in 81 BC, debating the wisdom of reform programs which had been put in place by the government, the authors were disturbed by the ostentatious display of wealth by the elite citizens of Chang'an. They wrote:

> ...you could see their carriages drawn up in rows, gleaming in gold or silver, and fitted with every sort of gadget. The horses themselves were neatly decked and shod, caparisoned with breast plates and pendant jewelry. They were kept in check by means of gilt or painted bits, with golden or inlaid bridles; and the not so rich made do with lacquered leather equipment or tassels.[10]

While chariots had become impractical as military vehicles, they obviously still maintained a role as a status symbol.

It seems almost certain that the ceremonial royal chariot hunt came to China along with the first chariots during the Shang dynasty. This is shown on inscribed oracle bones dating from the period of Shang ruler Wuding. By the end of the first millennium BC, imperial chariot hunts had become impressive ritual affairs that involved the massacre of great numbers of animals to demonstrate the ruler's potency. After the invention of the stirrup made riding a more dignified form of transport, the saddle soon deposed the chariot as the royal means of conveyance. Nevertheless, the ceremonial royal hunt would continue throughout the entire imperial period.

Chinese Harnessing Systems

One of the greatest inventions in Chinese and for that matter world history, was the breast-strap harnessing system for horses. This probably occurred during the late Warring States period around 300 BC.

Early Ox and Throat-and-Girth Horse Harness

Throughout the world, oxen were harnessed prior to horses. Horses, however, have greater endurance and can generate fifty percent more foot-pounds per second than oxen because of their greater speed. As such, man was quite anxious to harness their power shortly after domestication. When humans first attempted to harness the power of the horse, it was quite logical that they looked for a model in the highly successful yoke-based system used with oxen. The physiology of the two animals, however, is quite different. The neck of an ox extends from the body horizontally, quite unlike the sloping neck of a horse. Also, the ox's spinal column forms a bony hump in front of which a yoke can effectively be placed.

The traditional ox harnessing system, with the yoke on each side of a central pole or between shafts, was quite inappropriate for horses. As humans attempted to modify and adapt the existing ox system, the throat-and-girth system emerged as the first harnessing system for horses.

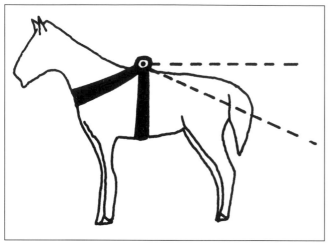

Figure 6

The throat-and-girth (Fig. 6) horse harness is made up of a girth circling the belly and the rear part of the ribs with the point of traction being located at the top. To prevent the girth slipping backwards, a throat strap was added. This crossed the withers diagonally and surrounded the throat of the animal, compressing the horse's trachea. The inevitable result was to suffocate the horse as soon as it attempted to pull against the harness.

Early in the twentieth century, a French cavalry officer, Lefebvre des Noëttes, became the first to investigate harness systems used in different cultures at different times, and to make actual reconstructions of the ancient systems used. In regards to the significance of the breast-strap harness he writes:

> The 'antique' harness, …(which we shall call throat-and-girth harness), could make use only of a small fraction of the possible motive force of each animal, failed to ensure satisfactory collective effort, and in general yielded a very low efficiency. The two [The throat-and girth and breast-strap systems] are so different that the former cannot possibly be interpreted as a variant of the latter, and cannot, indeed, have grown out of the latter. The throat-and-girth harness was a single clearly recognizable type, which remained unchanged from its first appearance in the most ancient illustrations we have, until it finally died out in the Middle Ages in Western Europe. And, moreover, it was the same everywhere, in every ancient realm and culture, equally inefficient. Only one ancient civilization broke away from this and developed an efficient harness - China.[11]

The magnitude of the acceptance of the throat-and-girth harnessing system, and of its staying power, is best summarized by Joseph Needham.

> The really astonishing thing about the throat-and-girth harness is the immense spread which it had both in space and time. We find it first in the oldest Chaldean representations from the beginning of the 3rd millennium BC onwards [and] in Sumeria and Assyria in -1400 to -800 [BC]. It was in sole use in Egypt from at least -1500 [BC], where it is shown on all paintings and carvings of chariots and horses, and it was likewise universal in Minoan and Greek times. Innumerable examples occur in Roman representations of all periods. The empire of the throat-and-girth system also covered Etruscan, Persian and early Byzantine vehicles without exception. Western Europe knew nothing else until about +600 [AD], nor did Islam. Moreover, the south of Asia was almost entirely in reliance on this inefficient harness, for it is seen in most of the pictures of carts which we have from ancient and medieval India, Java, Burma, Siam and other parts of that area. Central Asia, too, has it, e.g. at Bāmiyān. One of its last appearances occurs on a bas-relief of the +14th century at Florence in Italy, where it may be a conscious archaism.[12]

The equine throat-and-girth harness was very inefficient. The degree of this inefficiency was measured in 1910 by Lefebvre des Noëttes. He determined that two horses using throat-and-girth harness could pull about 1,100 pounds, or roughly one-half ton. On the other hand, des Noëttes' experiments showed that a single horse utilizing a modern collar-harness can easily pull a load of a ton and a half. As the pulling efficiency of the breast-strap harness system and collar system are virtually the same, it is possible to look at textual and archaeological evidence regarding the size and weight of Chinese vehicles to determine when the Chinese made the transition from throat-and-girth harness to the breast-strap system.

Transition to the Breast-strap Harnessing System

A study of Han dynasty representations of chariots and carriages, compared with those from all other ancient civilizations, clearly shows that the much heavier Chinese vehicles, carrying up to six people, could be pulled by a single horse. Much lighter vehicles from other parts of the world could carry a maximum load of two people but often required four horses. This could only be possible with a more efficient harnessing system which did not restrict the horse's ability to breath.

In the fourth century BC text, *Mozi* (*The Book of Master Mo*), a passage records the comments of Mo Di regarding a kite built by Gongshu Fan. The passage also gives us a good description as to the weight of Chinese vehicles of that time.

> Kungshu Phan [Gongshu Fan] constructed a bird from bamboo and wood, and when completed, it flew. For three days it stayed up in the air, and Kungshu [Gongshu] was proud indeed of his skill. But Mo Tzu [Mozi] said to him, 'Your achievement in constructing this bird is not comparable with that of a carpenter in making a linchpin [used to secure the wheels to a horse-drawn vehicle]. In a few moments he cuts out a piece of wood which, though only three inches long, can carry a load no less than fifty tan [dan] in weight [6,000 lbs. One dan equaled 120 lbs. in Warring States period]. Indeed, any achievement which is beneficial to man may be said to be skillful while anything not beneficial may be said to be clumsy.[13]

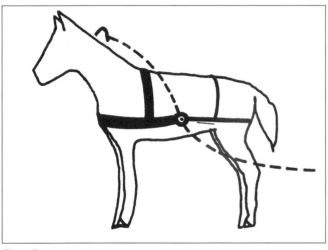

Figure 7

These figures certainly support the view that the breast-strap harness (Fig. 7) must have already been invented and in use by the late Warring States period (480-221 BC). In some cases, horses are even shown harnessed in tandem to shafted four-wheeled wagons. This arrangement would also have been impossible without the use of the breast-strap harness.

Based on the evidence, it seems logical to assume, that probably during the Warring States period, someone realized that the horse's shoulders could be surrounded by a trace. If this was suspended by a strap coming down from the withers and attached to the middle point of the curving vehicle shafts, it would greatly increase the efficiency of the animal's work. The continuation of the trace around the animal's hind-quarters, and its support by a hip-strap, was not a necessary part of the pulling mechanism, but allowed for the backward movement of the cart, and its braking when descending slopes.

How the Chinese were led to make one of the greatest breakthroughs in equestrian history is still a mystery. One theory holds that the invention of the breast-strap harnessing system for horses was derived from the human harness system used for boat haulage on China's canals and rivers. The hauling of boats upstream by large groups of men was an ancient practice in China. Men would have to have realized from their own experience that to be effective, pulling force must be exerted from the sternal and clavicular region in such a way as to permit free breathing.

After the invention of the breast-strap system, the yoke became virtually useless. Prior to the beginning of the Zhou dynasty it took the shape of a narrow "V" or wishbone. The lower ends of the yoke were turned up to act as reins guides. Around the Warring States period, the Chinese began to abandon the central pole in favor of straight shafts and the curving S-shaped shafts typical of the Han dynasty chariot. The shafts were originally connected above and behind the horse's neck by a crossbar. The yoke, while now serving no essential purpose, still persisted, probably as a guide for the reins. After the invention of the breast-strap harness and the attachment of the traces directly to the bend of the shafts, the crossbar and the forked yoke eventually disappeared. Since the breast-strap harness system would have been necessary in order for these vehicles to have been powered by a single horse, it is reasonable to assume that its invention preceded the shift to shafted carriages.

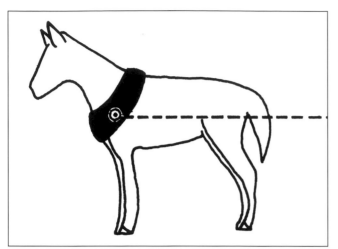

Figure 8

The Collar Harness

The Chinese invented the horse collar around the first century BC. Of all harnessing systems discussed, the collar harness was the most efficient. The original Chinese version of the collar harness is very similar to the modern harness systems of today. Robert Temple explains the genesis for this, the last of the great Chinese harnessing innovations.

> The earliest Chinese collar harness (Fig. 8) provided the horse with an artificial [ox-like] "hump", to which a yoke was then attached. In other words, the horse was transformed into an ox-substitute by the collar and the hump it created at the top of the horse's neck. The collar was padded to avoid rubbing and causing sores on the horse's back.

> The earliest evidence for the collar harness in China may be seen in a rubbing from an ancient brick, showing the collar harness on three horses pulling a chariot. It dates from some time between the fourth and first centuries BC. Therefore, we must consider the collar harness as having been invented in China by the first century BC at the latest.[14]

First Horseback Riding in China

While it is hard to say with any certainty when the horse was first ridden in China, it is felt that the Chinese had acquired a form of the saddle by the seventh century BC, and that cavalry first appeared during the Warring States period. By the Han dynasty mounted cavalry had become the dominant military use of the horse. Riding astride, however, had been practiced along the northern border and in several of the Eastern Zhou feudal states in the north, long before the adoption of mounted warfare.

The most important Chinese appropriation from its nomadic neighbors, however, was horseback riding and mounted warfare. The similarity of saddles and bridles shown on cavalry horses of Qin Shi Huang's "terracotta army" and of those found at the southern Siberian site at Pazyryk (fifth century BC) demonstrates the Chinese debt to the mounted tribes of the Eurasian steppes. This holds true not only for the technology of riding astride, but also for the riding gear that made this practical.

Horse bits specifically designed for riding and dating to as early as the sixth century BC, have been found in northern Shanxi Province and in non-Chinese tombs at Jundushan, Yanqing County, north of Beijing. This type of bit has a jointed mouthpiece with stirrup-shaped end loops through which leather straps attached the cheek pieces. Similarly designed bits were used throughout the Eurasian steppes in the eighth or seventh century BC. The earliest of these had snaffle bits and cheek pieces with three attachment holes. During the sixth century BC, the number of holes in the cheek pieces was reduced to two. In the sixth or fifth century BC, the Scythians, one of the great early equestrian cultures, developed a more secure method of attaching the cheek piece to the bit whereby each end of the mouthpiece ended with a large loop. An S-shaped cheek piece was then fitted into the loop. This type of bit and bridle was introduced into China during the late Eastern Zhou period and can be seen on the cavalry horses from the Emperor Qin Shi Huang's mausoleum.

The Chinese were reluctant riders. China was an agrarian country, quite unlike the pastoral culture practiced by its neighbors. The average Chinese farmer was generally not raised with a great familiarity of horses. For draught work on a farm, oxen were much more economical to feed and keep. In addition, China's chronic horse shortages often resulted in the ownership or usage of horses being restricted to government and court officials and the military. In comparison, children within the nomadic cultures to the north, by necessity, would have to acquire basic riding skills almost as soon as they could walk. Even the long robes traditionally worn by the Chinese presented a serious barrier to riding astride.

Figure 9

Mounted Cavalry Replace Chariot Forces

As stated previously, the Chinese adoption of cavalry warfare is generally dated to the Warring States period (Fig. 9). This coincides with the rise of the Xiongnu as a formidable mounted force and with their ever-increasing raids into China. (Most historians have held that the Xiongnus and the Huns were synonymous. In recent years, this theory has been challenged by the noted Chinese historian, Jacques Gernet.) *The Records of the Historian* and the *Intrigues of the Warring States* record that in 307 BC, King Wu Ling of the state of Zhao, in an effort to improve the military effectiveness of his troops in interstate warfare, decreed that Zhao soldiers should wear nomadic dress and ride astride in battle. For the time and culture this was a revolutionary proclamation. While the Chinese considered their land the place "where all things of value and utility are assembled," it seems obvious that they acknowledged that when it came to horses, those to the west or the north, and even those of their nomadic enemies, were superior.[15]

Linguistic evidence, especially the increasing use of the word "*qi*" - to ride astride - and "*an*" - the saddle - supports the supposition that riding was taking on a greater prominence by the end of the Warring States period. The late Western Han dynasty text, *Discourses on Salt and Iron*, refers to a fully formed saddle with cantle and fork. During the Han a variety of types of saddles, saddle pads, and saddlecloths coexisted, from small pads to large and flamboyant saddlecloths made of leather and, in some cases, saddles formed around a solid wooden tree. By the end of the Han dynasty, a military saddle had been developed that supported the hips and upper legs. In all likelihood, this was to provide stability for a spear throwing mounted rider. Prior to the invention of the stirrup, this would have provided a tremendous advantage to the rider in combat.

Sun Bin's <u>The Art of Warfare</u>: Cavalry Warfare

In approximately 350 BC, the effective use of cavalry in war is discussed in some detail in the military treatise *The Art of Warfare* accredited to Sun Bin, a descendant of the great military theorist, Sunzi. In the introduction of the 1996 translation by D. C. Lau and Roger T. Ames, the authors discuss how the growth of cities in China, and therefore their growth as targets for invading armies, had fundamentally changed the nature of war.

> Over a relatively short period of time, the straightforward and more decisive clash of war chariots and loose infantry dispatched from population centers to the flatlands that divided them, had given way to deployment of increasingly large infantries and mounted cavalries, and to the protracted siege of walled cities....

> Another innovation in warfare during this period was the rapid spread of cavalry as a complement to the infantry and the archers, having as it does an entirely different capability on the field of battle. When cavalry was introduced in the mid-fourth century BC through the example of the northern barbarians, there was considerable reluctance on the part of the Chinese kingdoms to adopt that mode of warfare, especially on account of the unsightly apparel that made it feasible... While there is no mention at all of cavalry in the thirteen "core" chapters of *Suntzu [Sunzi]*, it does appear in a number of the passages from the encyclopedic literature that have traditionally been ascribed to Sun Wu...[16]

As is shown below, *Sun Bin*, unlike *Sunzi*, devotes considerable attention to cavalry tactics.

> *Sun Pin* [Bin] 7: Divide the chariots and cavalry that will be used in combat into three detachments: one on either flank and one at the rear. On flat and easy ground, make greater use of the war chariots; on rugged terrain use more cavalry; on terrain that is sheer and closes in on both sides, use more cross-bowmen.

> *Sun Pin* [Bin] *18*: He (the student of military strategy) asked, "The two armies have drawn their battle lines and are ready for contest. We have the infantry advantage, but we are outnumbered in chariots and cavalry by ten to one. How should we attack this enemy?"

> Sun Pin [Bin] replied, "To attack an enemy under these conditions, we should keep to the steep and narrow ground and cautiously avoid flat, open terrain. This is because where the terrain is flat, the advantage belongs to the chariots, but on steep ground, the advantage belongs to the foot soldiers. This is the way (*tao*) [*dao*] to attack an enemy's chariot force."[17]

Sun Bin also addresses the *Ten Advantages of Using Cavalry* in a passage recovered from the Tang dynasty encyclopedia, *Tongdian*.

> Sun Pin [Bin] said, The use of the cavalry has ten advantages. The first is engaging the enemy when he first arrives. The second is taking advantage of the enemy when his back is unsupported. The third is giving chase to the scattered and attacking the disorderly. The fourth is striking the enemy's rear when engaging him and thus putting him to flight. The fifth is intercepting enemy provisions and cutting off his communication lines. The sixth is destroying his landings and passes and razing his bridges and trestles. The seventh is taking him by surprise where he is unprepared and making unexpected attacks on him before he can group himself. The eighth is attacking him when he is lax and going by way of places where it would never occur to him you would go. The ninth is burning his stores and emptying his markets and his villages. The tenth is plundering his fields and his countryside and carrying his youths off in bondage.

> These ten are the advantages of cavalry warfare. The cavalry is able to split off and to join, to scatter and to gather. It can turn up at a rendezvous a hundred or even a thousand li away. It goes out and returns without interruption, and thus is called a "force that can split off and join."[18]

Invention of the Stirrup (ca. AD 322)

With the emergence of cavalry as an important element of warfare, the major limiting factor on its effectiveness had been the lack of a secure seat from which the rider could fight. For this reason, the invention of the stirrup ranks as one of the most important equestrian discoveries in history. Why it would take so long to evolve after man first learned the arts of riding, is still a mystery. The stirrup transformed a horse's back into a secure fighting platform. Without it, there could be no really effective heavy cavalry. Its invention by the Chinese ranks as one of their most important contributions to world culture.

Prior to the stirrup, horsemen were forced to hold tightly to the horse's mane to avoid falling off when galloping or jumping. A handhold on their saddles provided the Romans a measure of stability, but their legs still dangled at the sides if not tightly pressed to the horses' flanks.

The stirrup was not an overnight invention, and owes its final evolution to a variety of attempts to stabilize the rider. It also had the effect of making mounting a horse safer and easier. Prior to the stirrup, mounting a horse, particularly while carrying weapons, could be a risky business. In 522 BC, it is recorded that the Persian King Cambyses fatally impaled himself on his own weapon while attempting to mount his horse. Skilled riders took pride in their flying leaps, gripping the mane with the left hand and swinging themselves up onto the horse's back. Ancient cavalrymen often used their spears to help them mount, either by pole-vaulting, or by using a peg sticking out of the spear as a step.

In India, during the late second century BC, one of the earliest stabilization devices appeared in the form of the surcingle (saddle strap or girth), behind which riders would tuck their feet. Soon after, it is thought that the Indians also invented the first "toe" stirrup. This was no more than a flexible loop of rope or leather through which the big toe was inserted. The reason that a larger version of the toe stirrup, able to accommodate the entire foot, failed to gain favor was the fact that if the rider should fall from his mount with such a stirrup wrapped around his foot, he would in all likelihood be dragged to death. One of the main drawbacks of the toe stirrup was that it was particularly unsuited to colder climates.

The Evolution of the True Stirrup

It is now believed that the first true stirrup was developed not to increase the stability of the rider, but to provide him with an easier and safer method for mounting his horse. The mounting stirrup did not come in pairs, and was attached to only one side of the saddle. The earliest documented example of a mounting stirrup was discovered on a pottery figure of a cavalryman in a Western Jin dynasty (265-316) tomb dating from 302 near Changsha.

The earliest depiction of a pair of riding stirrups was discovered on a pottery horse at a tomb near Nanjing dating from 322. The stirrups shown on the Nanjing horse were triangular in shape and provide the world's first known representation of a pair of riding stirrups. The first actual stirrup was discovered in a Xianbei site near Anyang in 1974. This was a single stirrup thought to date from the fourth century.

From the fourth century onward, the stirrup had spread to North China, northeast Asia, farther south into Korea, and even into Japan. In all of these locations, stirrups were oval and flat, and with a rather long handle, with either a wooden core covered by gilded bronze or iron plate or forged entirely from bronze or iron.

The expertise in metal casting which the Chinese had mastered over an millennium before, made it possible for them to cast the stirrups at a prodigious rate, thus speeding their spread throughout China and beyond.[19]

Horse Armor: From the Three Kingdoms Period to the Tang Dynasty

Most of the information we have regarding horse armor has come from figurines and frescoes, as there have been virtually no discoveries of intact armor through excavations. The first documented use of horse armor in China dates from the Three Kingdom period (220-265). During the Western Jin dynasty, the use of horse armor (*ju zhuang kai*) began to increase.

Excellent depictions of horse armor have been found in cave frescoes at Dunhuang dating from the Western Wei period (535-566). Color images found on molded bricks unearthed from the tombs at Dengxian, Henan Province, show armor covering the whole horse with the exception of its ears, mouth, legs and tail. A cavalryman is also shown in full armor riding on a horse in armor. These riders were referred to as "double armored cavalrymen (*jia qi ju zhuang*)."

Horse armor of the period consisted of six parts - the face mask (*mian lian*), the neck plate (*ji jing*), the breastplate (*dang xiong*), the trunk plate (*ma shen jia*), the buttocks or rump plate (*da hou*), and a part which was placed vertically on the rump of the horse (*jisheng*). Suits of equine armor like their human counterparts were made of iron or leather. The leather armor was often painted in bright colors or to resemble the coat of a tiger.

The use of horse armor continued to grow during the Sui dynasty (589-618), but was essentially the same in form as that of the Northern dynasties. Armor's growth is demonstrated by the pottery figurines of armored cavalrymen on armored horses unearthed from the tomb of Li He dating 582, and from the tomb of Liu Wei dating from 583. Military units and their horses would all wear armor of the same material (either leather or iron) and of the same color. In a description from the *History of the Sui Dynasty* of the Sui expedition to Liao Dong in 611, each Sui army was said to have had four regiments of cavalry. Two of the regiments were equipped with iron armor and two with leather armor, with the first regiment's iron armor and iron horse armor threaded with black silk cord and decorated with black tassels. The second regiment had red leather armor and red leather horse armor threaded with red silk cord and decorated with red tassels. The third regiment wore white iron armor for both men and horses, which was threaded with white silk cord and decorated with white tassels. The fourth regiment sported black leather armor and black leather horse armor threaded with black silk cord, and decorated with black tassels.

By the Tang dynasty (618-907), the popularity of horse armor had greatly decreased. The few available pottery figures displaying armor are, for the most part, brightly painted and often highlighted with strips of gold.[20]

The Qin Dynasty

The Qin people, who would eventually establish China's first dynasty, moved into the Wei River Valley from the west and were noted for their skill with horses. Due to their equestrian prowess, people of the Qin were recruited to drive the carriages of Zhou royalty. Legend states that King Mu of the Zhou hired a Qin driver who was once ordered by the King to drive his eight-horse carriage to the Kunlun Mountains far to the West. While there, the King received word of a rebellion in the capital city of Haojing. It was said that the driver, realizing the urgency of the situation, drove his horses at a rate of "one thousand li" (one li = 1/3 mile) per day.

At the time Qin Shi Huang united China and established the first dynasty, the Qin possessed many forms of vehicles. Among these were:

> ....a deluxe carriage drawn by six horses used by the emperor (*jin'gen-che*), an imperial carriage (*nian-che*), a small carriage with seats, painted in five colors (*wuse an-ch*e), a carriage in which the occupants rode standing up (*li-che*), a carriage for attendants (*shu-che*), a light carriage (*you-che*), a small war chariot (*xiao-rong*), and a general road vehicle (*lu-che*).[21]

Figure 10

Light Cavalry in the Qin Dynasty

Based on the excavation of the Qin Shi Huang mausoleum, Albert Dien noted the following regarding the Qin Cavalry.

> The evidence we have indicates that cavalry in China was of the "light" variety until at least the fourth century AD. The traditional date for the adoption of mounted archery in China is 307 BC, but the first real evidence with respect to equipment and appearance is probably the extraordinary pottery figures from the mausoleum complex of Qin Shihuang [Qin Shi Huang]. The second of the three pits thus far reported is estimated to contain 16 figures of cavalrymen and mounts [Fig. 10]. The armor worn by the mounted soldiers is shorter than that of the armored infantrymen and has no shoulder guards. The robes worn under the armor also differ from those of the foot soldiers in that the overlap is to the front,

probably to facilitate riding. The cavalrymen wear small caps with chinstraps and are shod in boots rather than in sandals. They are believed to have been archers, since their left hands seem to have held bows, and quivers holding eighty to a hundred arrows each were found in their vicinity. The military array of the pottery figures calls to mind the description in the *Zhanguoce [Intrigues of the Warring States]* of the Qin army of one million warriors wearing armor, one thousand chariots, and ten thousand cavalry. The ratio supports what the pits seem to indicate that the cavalry at that time was a relatively minor part of the military force.[22]

The Han Dynasty
Introduction of New Horse Breeds to China

Once the Chinese made the transition to riding and cavalry replaced chariots as the major force in warfare, the importation of horses superior to native stock became a much higher priority. The Xiongnu controlled a vast area stretching from Manchuria in the west to Turkestan in the east, and posed a serious threat to the Chinese. With increasingly frequent raids into China by the Xiongnu, the need for the Chinese to secure finer horses became even greater. Around 160 BC, Zhao Zu, a Chinese official, commented that "the territory [of the Xiongnu], and the skills it demands, are different from those of China. In climbing up and down mountains and crossing ravines and mountain torrents, the horses of China cannot compare with those of the Hsiung-nu [Xiongnu]."[23]

The search for superior horses and for allies against the Xiongnu led to one of the more interesting chapters in China's equestrian history - the incredible journey of Zhang Qian and the resulting campaign to obtain premium horses from the land of Ferghana. While these events were significant in their own right, the ultimate result - the opening of the Silk Roads - would prove to be one of the more significant occurrences in Chinese history.

The Search for Better Horses

During the reign of Emperor Wendi (r. 180-157 BC), raids into China by the Xiongnu increased, with scouts coming within view of the capitol in 166 BC. Upon assuming the throne, Han Emperor Wudi (r. 140 to 87 BC) initiated a vigorous campaign which drove the Xiongnu back into the Gobi desert. This proved incredibly expensive with up to 100,000 cavalrymen being killed in a single battle. Although this provided temporary relief from the nomadic raiding, the Chinese needed better horses if they were to bring long-term stability to their borders. While Wudi's efforts to obtain the "heavenly horses" of Ferghana (Dayuan) may well be the most famous Chinese effort to secure superior horses, it was certainly not the only attempt.

The Western Journey of Zhang Qian

Emperor Wudi was interested in establishing alliances with western states hostile to the Xiongnu. In 138 BC, the Emperor sent his envoy, Zhang Qian, on a diplomatic mission to forge an alliance with the Yuezhi tribe, which had been forced west by the Xiongnu. Zhang's journey covered more than 3,000 kilometers and took some 12 years, including time spent as a captive of the Xiongnu. Zhang Qian was finally successful in finding the Yuezhi in what is now Afghanistan; however, their King had no interest in further fighting against the Xiongnu.

While Zhang was unsuccessful in his attempt to strike an alliance with Yuezhi, he returned to the Han court with a greatly expanded knowledge of the lands which lay to the west of China. One item in particular caught the attention of Emperor Wudi. Zhang reported that in the land of Ferghana (modern Turkmenistan), he had encountered amazingly fine horses that sweated blood. The "blood sweating" resulted from a parasite (Parofiliaria multipupillosa) that infested the horses. When the horses were active, small amounts of blood mixed with the sweat to form a pink foam. In all likelihood, these horses were early ancestors of the modern Turanian and the Akhal-Teké breeds.

These horses and horsemen had been referred to earlier in history. During the fourth century BC, when Alexander the Great reached Margiana in southern Turkmenistan, he met fierce resistance from nomadic Sacae and Massagetae tribes that already employed the stiff saddle and were skilled in cavalry tactics. Descriptions of their horses were very similar to those encountered in Ferghana by Zhang Qian.

The early nomads of the steppe had, out of necessity, developed their knowledge of horse breeding. The Scythian warhorses found preserved in frozen tombs at Pazyryk in the Altai Mountains show that as early as 500 BC they had produced tall, fast horses, very similar to the modern Akhal-Teké. "These warhorses of Central Asia were famous throughout the ancient world. At different times and places, they were called either Bactrian, Sogdian, Median, Parthian, Hyrcanian, or Chorasmian."[24]

There is little doubt that the horses of Ferghana were of much greater stature than those of the Chinese. During the first century AD, a Chinese court official wrote that they stood "all seven ch'ih [chi] in height" (63.66 inches or almost 16 hands). This is considerably taller than the 13.2 hand horses found with the Qin Shi Huang terra-cotta army. Even during the Song dynasty (960- 279), nearly a millennium later, military horses bought by the Chinese government stood only up to 57.73 inches, or 14.2 hands.[25]

Archaeological excavations in Yangjiawan, Shaanxi Province, from the second century BC produced two groups of miniature horses and riders made of gray earthenware. One group contains horses with angular bodies, standing nearly 27 inches in height. The other group comprised horses with rounder bodies and measuring approximately 20 inches in height.

> The discovery at Yangjiawan shows that large horses, probably acquired from the Xiongnu, with whom the Chinese had both military and commercial contact beginning in the third century BC, were already available to the Chinese well before the presentation of either the Wu sun [Wusun] or the Ferghana horses to Emperor Wudi. The smaller Yangjiawan horses may depict an imported horse of lesser quality or a crossbreed between imported and local horses, such as those represented by figurines found in Sichuan.[26]

Emperor Wudi was intrigued with Zhang's report both because of China's military need for horses of high quality, and also because he felt that these horses might be the legendary "heavenly horses" which could be the vehicle to his own immortality. In Chinese mythology, the horse and dragon are closely related in that both are purported to have the ability to fly and carry their riders to the home of the immortals. Horses with this capability were referred to as "heavenly horses" (tian ma). Han Wudi had been told that "the divine horse" (shen ma) would come from the northwest, and felt that if he could acquire one of these horses, it would bear him to immortality, as had the horse of the mythical Yellow Emperor.[27]

The War of the Heavenly Horses

Whether motivated by China's chronic need for superior cavalry stock, or by the quest for his own immortality, Han Wudi launched the first of several military missions to secure the "heavenly horses" in 104 BC, after the ruler of Ferghana had not only refused to sell their prize horses to the Chinese, but also murdered the envoys sent to purchase them. Wudi ordered Li Guangli, commander of the border post of Dunhuang, to proceed west to Ferghana with an army of 6,000 cavalry and 20,000 soldiers to take the horses by force. The rigors of the journey through hostile mountains and deserts resulted in the death of more than half of the expeditionary force. The depleted and exhausted Chinese troops were defeated badly. After two years, the remainder of the force returned to the Chinese border and to a furious Emperor.

In 101 BC, despite protests that the country could not afford another costly campaign, Han Wudi ordered that Li Guangli return to Ferghana with a larger army. The expeditionary force consisted of some 60,000 soldiers and 30,000 horses, along with engineers, porters and attendants. To sustain them on the long march, they also assembled a herd of more than 100,000 cattle. Despite the loss of half of the army on the difficult march, Ferghana submitted to the superior Chinese force when the Ferghanan king was murdered by his own citizens after a 40-day siege. He was replaced by a king favorable to the Chinese, and Ferghana became a vassal state of the Han. Li Guangli was able to collect some 3,000 horses for his Emperor, but only a small percentage of these were the superior horses sought by Han Wudi. On the arduous return journey more than 2,000 of the horses died. By the time they reached the capital, only fifty of the "blood sweating" horses and around 1,000 inferior quality horses had survived.

As the horses neared Chang'an in 101 BC, there was great excitement throughout the city. The following sacrificial hymn, possibly written by Han Wudi himself, was sung in anticipation of their arrival.

> The Heavenly Horses are coming,
> Coming from the Far West.
> They crossed the Flowing Sands,
> For the barbarians are conquered.
> The Heavenly Horses are coming
> That issued from the waters of a pool.
> Two of them have tiger backs:
> They can transform themselves like spirits.
> The Heavenly Horses are coming
> Across the pastureless wilds
> A thousand leagues at a stretch,
> Following the eastern road.
> The Heavenly horses are coming.
>
> Jupiter is in the Dragon,
> Should they choose to soar aloft,
> Who could keep pace with them?
> The Heavenly Horses are coming
> Open the gates while there is time.
> They will draw me up and carry me
> To the Holy Mountain of K'un-lun [Kunlun].
> The Heavenly Horses have come
> And the Dragon will follow in their wake.
> I shall reach the Gates of Heaven,
> I shall see the Palace of God.[28]

Regarding the song and the possible religious motivation for Han Wudi's extraordinary efforts to acquire the "heavenly horse," Arthur Waley states:

> Whether the people of Ferghana believed that their sacred horses "issued from a pool" we do not know, but there are...many Chinese stories of horses coming up out of the water, the implication being that they are dragon-horses, that is to say, water dragons who have changed themselves into horses, often retaining their dragon wings. As we shall see, the Emperor had been on the lookout for a water-born horse for some time...
>
> The general implication of the hymn therefore is that the Heavenly Horses will carry the Emperor to the abode of the Immortals on the magical mountain Kunlun...
>
> ...the Emperor's search for immortality did not begin with his interest in divine horses. He had sent numerous and costly expeditions to the East in the hope of discovering islands inhabited by Immortals who might be persuaded to yield their secrets to him. He had dabbled in alchemy, in the belief that if he ate out of vessels made of alchemic gold he would live forever, or at any rate for a prodigiously long

time. The expedition to fetch magic horses from the West was, it seems to me, merely a continuation of his earlier quests in the East. 'The Emperor Wu,' says Wen Ying in about AD 200, 'had set his heart on immortality. He was always hoping that a Heavenly Horse would come and carry him to Kunlun,' the western Abode of the Immortals. At last when all his quests in the East had failed and when the Horse did not come of its own accord (as it had come to the legendary Emperors in the past, both in India and in China) he determined, having known for long that the king of Ferghana had such horses, to wrest some from him by diplomacy or, if need be, by force.[29]

In reality, Han Wudi's motivation for launching the second campaign against Ferghana was almost surely multi-fold. China's chronic problem in securing quality horses for their struggles against their northern neighbors obviously played a major role, as did Han Wudi's quest for immortality. Also requiring consideration though, was Han Wudi's desire to expand his empire and thus his own fame, and the fact that the reputation of the Chinese nation and its emperor had been seriously eroded by the disastrous defeat on the first sojourn to Ferghana, a fact that could create serious future problems with China's neighbors. No doubt, as a result of China's subjugation of Ferghana, other states in the Tarim Basin voluntarily submitted to the Han court and the influence of the Empire was expanded. Within a short period of time, Chinese garrisons were established throughout the western region. In essence, this resulted in the establishment of regular contact between East and West, and the opening of the famous "Silk Roads." The other result, however, was an Empire left near bankrupt by the enormity of the expense of the two campaigns.

The Horses of the Wusun

In 115 BC, Zhang Qian was sent on a second mission by Emperor Wudi. South of Lake Balkhash in the Yili River valley, he encountered the Wusun, who also possessed horses that were larger and more refined than those of the Chinese. These are thought to be a cross between the horses of Ferghana and the Mongolian-type pony. As a result of Zhang Qian's mission, the Han court, on two occasions, received a large number of the Wusan horses in tribute. While the Wusan horses were not as strong nor as large as those from Ferghana, they were superior to the Chinese native stock.

The historical records, *Shiji*, by Sima Qian, also spoke of the introduction of western horses into China. During this period Wudi sent between five and ten trade missions annually to the states of Aorsi in the Yili valley, Yuezhi, and Parthia, as well as the more famous excursions to Ferghana. They exchanged Chinese silk and metal goods for horses, jade, coral and other luxury articles.

The Kuai Ti Horses

In 237 BC, an imperial edict was issued calling for the expulsion from the State of Qin of all ministers who were not native. Minister Li Si, who himself would be subject to dismissal by the ruling, argued that to reject all that was foreign would deprive Qin of many valuable and desirable things. He stated that "if only those things produced in Qin were to be permitted, then the women of Zheng and Wei would not occupy the rear palaces, and fine horses and *kuai ti* (swift horse) would not fill the outer stables."[30] This statement indicates that the Qin had obtained at least a certain number of the horses a century and a half prior to Han Emperor Wudi's acquisition of the "blood sweating" horses of Ferghana.

Around 100 BC, Sima Qian wrote that the Xiongnu possessed two types of excellent and rare horses. One was probably the Ferghana horse. Of the other, he wrote that a foal of this type was "able on the third day after its birth to jump over its mother."[31] This also appears to refer to the *kuai ti*.

By the end of the Han dynasty, the horse, particularly in its relationship to effective cavalry, had emerged as a major force in both the survival and the expansion of the Chinese State. H. G. Creel summarizes the period as follows:

By virtue of it [the horse], the nomads had become a deadly threat and were able at times to invade Chinese territory almost at will. The Chinese had to develop cavalry to counter the nomads, and even though they made great economic sacrifices to breed cavalry horses they still had to secure additional mounts from outside their borders. Both to secure horses and to outflank the Xiongnu, they pushed far into Central Asia, opening a new chapter in China's political and military history and in its foreign relations.[32]

The Non-Military Horse

As mentioned earlier, elaborate carriages and matched teams of fine horses were status symbols among the rich during the Han, particularly in the capital, Chang'an. With a population over one million, this was one of the largest and most diverse cities in the world.

Peasant farmers had little or no direct contact with horses during the Han rule. This was principally a matter of economics. In one day, a single horse consumed as much grain as an ordinary family of six. As a result, oxen were much more widely used in Chinese agriculture. Farm produce was conveyed from the fields by ox carts, and asses may have sometimes been used to pull a wagon.

Aside from agriculture, the Han established an elaborate system of imperial highways. Officials were allowed to use the highways, but were restricted from using the center lane, which was specially leveled and reserved for use by members of the royal court. The Han government also maintained a series of posts, each stocked with the necessary inventory of horses, which were used by officials to maintain contact, and impart the wishes of the Han court throughout the empire.[33]

Burial Processions and Vehicles of the Eastern Han Dynasty

Barbara Banks, in her work, *The Magical Powers of the Horse as Revealed in the Archaeological Explorations of Early China*, gives an excellent description of the horse-drawn vehicles of the Eastern Han dynasty (AD 25- AD 220).

> There were very strict rules governing the makeup of the official processions and the types of chariots that could be used by various officials. The chariot system was established in 145 BC and is recorded in the History of the *Later Han (Dynasty)*…
>
> There are at least six distinct types of chariots seen in the Han (mortuary) reliefs. The first is the *fu* or axe chariot. It is a chariot box with a vertically placed battle axe in the center. It is lightweight. The *Yufuzhi [Treatise on Transport]* from the *Hou Hanshu [History of the Later Han]* says: "The lightweight chariot… is the ancient war chariot … it is without cloth or top."
>
> The second type of chariot is the zhao chariot. It has the same kind of chariot box as the fu chariot, seemingly a horizontal rectangular shape. The front part of the chariot box is sloped for protection, the back part has no board railing. The chariot has an umbrella shaped canopy to cover and protect those within. Those seated within the *zhao* chariot can keep a lookout at will…
>
> The *shi fan* chariot's floor has four foundation posts that are connected with the chariot cover's tassels. Perhaps it is for this reason that the *Yufuzhi* refers to them as "four bonds," raising and propping up, adding strength to the functions of the chariot cover.
>
> The *zi* chariot and the *ping* chariot have the same overall shape. They have square chariot boxes, both sides of the two types of chariots have fabric shades, the chariot cover is large and the edge is rolled slightly upward. But the two types are not the

same. The *zi* chariot's shafts are relatively long, and a stepping platform is used when entering and disembarking. Both of these chariots are tall and are used by both men and women.

The *zhan* chariot is made of wood and bamboo. Both wood and bamboo are used to make the shed or awning of the chariot so it is also referred to as a shed or peng chariot. This type of chariot has a relative long box. The side railing boards on top of the frame rise, meet at the top, and form the awning or shed.

It is recorded in both the *Jingdingji* of the *Hanshu* and the *Yufuzhi* (Treatise on Transport) from the Hou Hanshu (History of the Later Han) that the Han chariot system was started in 145 BC. It is as follows:

1. Those (officials) above the 60 picul rode the *shi fan* chariot.
2. The wives of officials of the 2,000 picul rank and above rode the *zi* and the *peng* chariots.
3. County generals and those above them could add the *fu* chariot in front of their processions.
4. The empress dowager, the empress, the crown prince, princes, and imperial grandsons, all drove three horses. The emperor's sisters, princesses, noblemen including those ranked as the Three Lords and the Nine Nobles... [that is] 2,000 picul officials all drove two horses.
5. Officials earning 300 piculs and above have an honor guard of three chariots in antis and two chariots following them. The "Five officials under the gate" are divided before and after the master's chariot.[34]

[Picul-any of various units of weight used in China and southeast Asia; esp: a Chinese unit equal to 133.33 pounds or 60.477 kg.]

Horses and the Silk Trade

During the Han dynasty, silk served as the de facto currency, particularly in commercial dealings with the nomadic herdsmen on China's border. As early as the Qin, the Chinese were trading silk for horses with the Xiongnu. During this period, the arrangement seemed to favor the Chinese who felt that they were trading a non-essential luxury item for desperately needed mounts for their cavalry. A Chinese official noted during the first century BC, "Thus a single length of plain silk secures from the Xiongnu goods worth many pieces of gold, thus draining away the resources of our enemy."[35] Silk for horses, and later tea for horses, became a common practice throughout the majority of the imperial period. Over time, as the Chinese became more desperate for horses, the advantage in these dealings made a definite shift in favor of the nomadic herdsmen.

The Tang Dynasty

The Tang dynasty (618-907) stands as the one of the greatest periods in Chinese history. Thanks in part to stability along the Silk Roads, Chang'an, the capital (present day Xi'an), once again became the largest and most cosmopolitan city in the world, boasting a population of more than one million inhabitants.

The founders of the Tang represented the aristocratic families from the Northwest that had intermarried with sinicized nomads (nomads who had been assimilated into Chinese society) from the border regions of Shanxi and Shaanxi provinces. As such, they represented the most horse-oriented group to control the Chinese Empire to date.

The early Tang was a period of tolerance marked by the infusion of many foreign ideas and religions. Chang'an was home to Muslim mosques, Jewish synagogues, and Nestorian Christian churches. Buddhism flourished, with temples, often supported by the state, located throughout the country. Communities of Sogdians, Uighurs, Turks and Tibetans flourished within Chang'an's walls, as well as official envoys from more than 300 countries. These peoples not only introduced exotic goods to China, but also new skills such as polo, music, dancing, metalworking, and medicine. The Tang emperors opened China to the world, encouraging both cultural and commercial exchange. Within a short time, Chang'an stood as the educational center for all of Asia.

Strong Chinese military garrisons along the Silk Roads ensured safe passage from Chang'an to Kashgar. This was the "grand period" of the Silk Roads. Large trading towns were established and flourished along the route to service the many caravans.

Figure 11

Women in the Tang Dynasty

The Tang, owing to their northern origins, were much more liberal than past dynasties regarding women. As in the Han dynasty, the use of horses during the Tang was limited to the military and court officials by royal edict in 667. Tang women traditionally enjoyed many more privileges than their southern counterparts, a fact that carried through to their participation in equestrian activities including polo and hunting from horseback.

Early in the Tang dynasty, women used smaller carriages pulled by oxen for transportation. By the middle of the dynasty they often traveled sitting in a palanquin (a conveyance, usually for one person, that consists of an enclosed litter borne on the shoulders of men by means of poles), or riding astride. When riding, they wore western clothing and used a wide brimmed hat (of central Asian origin) with a veil attached. The veil was eventually dropped.

Tang Military Horses

To the Tang, the horse was a symbol of status and power, as well as a military necessity. A Tang official once stated, after disease had killed more than 180,000 horses: "Horses are the military preparedness of the state; if heaven takes this away, the state will totter to a fall."[36] When Gaozu (r. 618 - 626) first assumed the mantle of "Son of Heaven" in 618, China's supply of horses on the ranges of Gansu was at a precariously low level of 5,000. By 668, this figure had dramatically increased to 706,000. An elaborate system of inspectorates (stud farms) was established in Gansu, Shanxi, and Shaanxi provinces, each containing 50,000 horses. New horses were branded, noting their specific herd, class of work, and origin. They were then assigned to a herd of 120.

The *Tang Lu shu* lists at least nine punishable offenses for those who might lose or abuse the government's horses. These include:
· overloading a post-horse
· riding a post-horse off the highway or passing a post-station without changing horses
· making a personal present of a post-horse temporarily in one's possession
· concealing private goods in a post-horse's baggage
· riding an unbroken government horse
· willfully slaughtering a government horse
· stealing and then slaughtering a government horse
· fabricating credentials to use a post-horse
· unauthorized use of a post-horse

The most serious of these offenses - stealing and then slaughtering a government owned horse - called for a sentence of two and a half years at hard labor.[37]

Reflecting their love for both horses and battle, the Tang cavalry was the domain of the elite. This was confirmed by a Tang edict mandating that cavalrymen supply their own horses and weapons, a task prohibitive for all but the wealthy. Peasants, who had little or no experience with horses, were recruited to serve in the infantry or to assist in producing crops necessary to keep the army fed.

Increased Horse Imports

Prior to the An Lushan rebellion in 754, the common Mongolian-type horses of the Chinese had been crossed with a variety of other breeds. These efforts were a continuation of those begun by Emperor Wudi with the Wusun, Yili River, and Ferghana horses during the Han dynasty. The Tang dynasty represented the apex of Chinese horse breeding programs with additional bloodstock coming from the central Asian states of Kokand, Samarkand, Bukhara, Kish, Chack, Maimargh, Khuttal, Gandhara, Khotan, and Kirghiz. In addition, in 703 it was noted that the royal court received several high quality Arab horses.[38]

Through the art of the period, one can see that the horses of the Tang were larger and heavier than those of previous periods. Virginia Bower offers the following description and speculation regarding their increased girth.

Figure 12
Courtesy of the Oriental Institute of the University of Chicago

> The most prized mounts for battle, hunting, and polo were quite large, perhaps sixteen hands. They had a heavier frame than today's thoroughbreds, yet their thin legs, agility, and lively manner made them different from present-day draft horses. A contemporary polo player was amazed that the "heavy" horses depicted in the mural in Crown Prince Zhanghuai's tomb could be so nimble. These Tang horses... have the same heavy body and "Roman" nose - quite different from today's classic Arabian horses - as the horses ridden by the Sasamans, and many authorities speculate that they were all descendants of the famous "imperial" Nisean breed of Achaemenid Persia (Fig. 12), as pictured at Persepolis.[39]

The Tang aristocracy's love for the horse was clearly visible in their art. This can be seen not only in their marvelous sancai ceramic steeds and paintings featuring the horse, but also in the reliefs of Emperor Taizong's six favorite horses incorporated into his tomb. Horses, particularly the exotic horses from outside of China's borders, were also celebrated in both literature and verse.

Polo

The Tang fascination with things foreign, particularly those emanating from the West, made polo highly fashionable. In the 670s, Peroz (or Firuz), the son of the last Sasanian emperor arrived in the capital of Chang'an. As this coincides with the first mention of polo in Tang China, it is possible that he introduced the game that had originated in his native Persia. There is, however, no direct proof of this.

Polo is vividly depicted in the art and artifacts of the time. Robert Harrist offers the following description:

> Tang dynasty bronze mirrors decorated with female polo players have been excavated in Jiangsu Province... Ceramic polo players fall into two categories: dynamic persons riding horses in full "flying gallop," generally with no support or stand; and elegant depictions of players frozen still, usually with all four or at least three of the horse's legs attached to a rectangular base.

> Foreigners were much in evidence in the art of seventh and eighth century China, as is shown by numerous bearded polo players. The facial features and coiffure of many equestrienne players also resemble those of female figurines of about this date. Furthermore, their riding costume, a fitted jacket with narrow lapels and skirt or trousers, is typical of the attire adopted by Tang women in the second half of the seventh and the early eighth century for riding.

The appearance of a foreign man and a Chinese woman together on a polo field would not have been considered a breach of propriety until later periods, when upper class women were strictly separated from men who were not close relatives. Furthermore, the introduction of foot binding during the Song dynasty rendered female participation in sports such as polo unlikely.[40]

An article from the Silk Road Foundation notes:

Figure 13

> Those qualities that had attracted Tang emperors and others to the sport - the challenge of managing horse and polo stick simultaneously, the excitement of speed, and the thrill of pursuit - inspired artists and craftsmen as well. Like the related subjects of mounted hunting and combat, polo offered an opportunity to depict fine horses, skilled athletes, and exciting confrontations (Fig. 13). The sport was associated with the lifestyle of the elite, and in the Islamic world it had links to a heroic, legendary past. So also it did in China, where the Tang dynasty was regarded as a golden age and polo a passionate pursuit.[41]

Polo was played not only by emperors, nobles, and women of the court, but also by military men and scholars. Age, whether young or old, also seemed not to be a limiting factor in participation. For those unable to afford or obtain horses, there were also versions played on donkeys and even on foot.

A story, recorded in the *Old Standard History of the Tang (Jiu Tang Shu)* during the tenth century by Liu Xu (887-946) and others, describes a match at a polo field within the palace. The occasion was the marriage of a Tang princess to a Tibetan king. Emperor Zhongzong (reigned 705-710) was asked by the Tibetan envoy if the Chinese could assemble a team to play against his countrymen. The Emperor agreed and fielded a four-man team, which included two of his sons and his nephew and future emperor, Xuanzong. The Tibetans were allowed ten players. The Chinese defeated the Tibetans and Xuanzong was highly praised for his skill and horsemanship.

Not all within the court were proponents of the game. Some saw polo as a waste of valuable time and also felt that it was a much too dangerous game for royal participation.

The Tang dynasty marked the apex of polo's popularity in China. While the Chinese may not have invented polo, they certainly enhanced its play with the invention of the stirrup and refinements they developed for the saddle. The game would survive into future dynasties, but never again would it be as popular or receive the royal patronage that it had during this period.

Equestrian Tack during the Tang Dynasty

Through the Northern and Southern dynasties (317-589), riding was mainly confined to the military. One reason may well have been that, prior to the use of the stirrup, riding was a rather undignified method of transportation. This would have been heightened by the lack of a fully developed saddle and other tack.

Owing to their northern tradition of riding, Tang men, including the emperor, not only made riding their primary means of transport, but also contributed greatly to the evolution of equestrian gear, accoutrements, and decoration. By the time of Emperor Zhongzong (r. 705-710), horseback riding had become a general custom, and equine equipment developed to a new state of completeness.

Sun Ji offers the following description of tack during the Tang dynasty.

> In ancient horse training, aside from the simple rope-harness (*shengtao*), the first true horse gear must have been the bridle (*luotou*). This originally lacked a bit

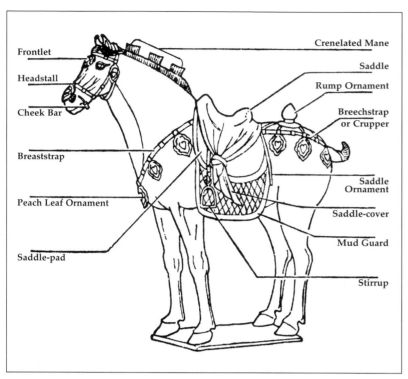

Figure 14

(*xian*) and cheek-bar (*biao*) as noted by a Tang commentary on the *Ji Jiu Pian*. The full unit, at the latest, dates from the Qin. The well-preserved articles from Pit 2 at the grave mound of Shihuang [Qin Shi Huang] comprise the neck-strap (*xiangdai*), brow-strap (*edai*), nose-band (*bidai*), throat-latch (*yandai*), and cheek-strap (*jiadai*). When the bridle was combined with the bit and the cheek-bars, one gained effective control over the horse's head. After this, major changes were not needed, and they were mainly ornamental in nature. Thus in Han times there was the brow ornament (*mayang*) also called *dan-glu*. In Tang times this was superseded by the apricot-leaf (*xingye*) ornament on the nose and upper cheeks. Other bridle ornaments are attested to in poems by Du Fu and Bai Juyi, and certain of these were to be used only by persons of rank.

The bit was called "that which is reined in" (*youle*) in Zhou bronze inscriptions, and the term *xian* is from the Han. In Han times the central iron piece in the horse's mouth was called the "arrowhead" (*di*). At each end were rings to which the bridle was connected, and these rings were pierced by the cheek-bars (*biao*). Horn bits have been found in several Eastern Zhou tombs. The cheek-bars were of various shapes, at times rather complicated.

In ancient times, like the Greeks, Romans, and border tribes, the Chinese did not use the saddle. However, certain terms found on bronze vessel inscriptions and in literary records suggest the use of a saddle-cloth or saddle. "*An*," which is defined by the *Shuo Wen Dictionary* as "a harnessing device for horses," appears in the *Zuo Zhuan*. Even though it serves here as a place name, "*an*" may have been applied to a place resembling a saddle, in which case China would have developed the saddle in the Spring and Autumn era [740-476 BC]. The cantles and saddlebows (*anqiao*) of the saddles represented on the Qin pottery figures and the Western Han figurines from Xianyang are relatively low. However, in the bronze equestrian objects found in Ding County, Hebei, the cantles and saddlebows become higher. These late Western Han [206 BC - AD 8] examples may be the "high cantles" referred to in the *San Fu Jue Lu*,... according to the *Chu Xue Ji*. At that time both cantles and saddlebows were high, but in Tang times the cantle was made to slant downward to facilitate mounting and dismounting. The saddles depicted on the six steeds of Zhao Ling and the ornamented saddles described in *Yuan 31* and *32* of the *Tang Hui Yao* all seem to have had an inner framework of wood.

Under the saddle was the *cun*, now called the saddle-pad (*anru*). It was generally made of felt, but there are references to pads of leather, tiger skin, and fur in Tang sources, and these are depicted on clay figurines from Tang tombs.

Under the pad was the mud-screen (*zhang ni*), dating from as early as the Three Kingdoms Period (*Sanguo*). During the Northern and Southern Dynasties it was often too long, e.g. for convenience in crossing rivers. Therefore in the Tang it was shortened.

When a horse equipped with saddle was not being ridden, the saddle was covered with a saddle-cover (*anfu*). This term and variants are found in Tang and Song sources.

In order to secure the saddle and saddle-pad it was necessary to run straps around the horse's chest, rump and belly. Below the saddle was the girth (*fudai*) in front was the breast-strap (*panxiong*); to the rear was the crupper (*qiu*). In addition to these utilitarian straps, the Tang added decorative straps behind the saddle to which jade and other ornamentation was applied. These resemble decorative elements found on depictions of Sassanian equestrian figures.

Other elements of decorative horse gear came during Tang times from foreign sources. An example is the "apricot leaf" (*xingye*), an ornament placed on the crupper, breast-strap and other harness which was influenced by Sassanian horse ornament. However, it also had Han antecedents in the pottery figurines found at Yangjiawan, Xianyang; and these in turn may have been influenced by the equestrian style found in the Altai at Pazyryk, which date from the fourth to the third century BC. Many floral and animal figures adorned these ornaments in Tang times.

An element of horse decoration during the Tang which may or may not be of foreign origin is the cutting of notches in the mane, typically leaving three tufts of hair, called "three flowers" (*sanhua*). There are many references to this practice in Tang and Song literature. There are many precedents for trimming the mane so as to leave one, two or more tufts, both in Chinese and foreign practice. This is indicated by Qin and Han examples as well as by the metal plaques of the steppe nomads. The Tang usage may have been influenced by the Turkish (*Tujue*) example.

Du Fu's "five flower horse" (*wuhua ma*) probably does not refer to a five-tufted mane as some have claimed, but rather the "curly hair" (*xuanmao*) attested by various sources.

There was also the practice of binding the tail (*fuwei*) during the Tang. This usage is attested by Han stone reliefs and literary sources. In Tang times it was also found among foreign countries such as the Sassanians.

These ornaments are referred to by various names in Tang poetry. In Song times the weight and pattern were determined by the rank of the rider.

One practice that was definitely of native origin was the "parasite" (*jisheng*), a kind of rump ornament often resembling a plant-like tassel. A case [an example] resembling a small tree is depicted in an Eastern Jin tomb in Yunnan, and a wall painting from Korea… shows a "parasite" as tall as a man. In Sui and Tang times the "fire pearl" (*huozhu*) also appeared in this position. This ornament was adopted by the Japanese as well, who called it "cloud pearl" (*yunzhu*). The "fire pearl" was probably related to the "parasite," but there are distinctions between them.

Some have written that horseshoes existed in China in Tang or pre-Tang times, but this is not supported by evidence. Probably horseshoes were not generally adopted in China until Yuan times.

China used the saddle and stirrup earlier than did the Western countries. Before the 4th century the latter only used a leg support (*qiaokou*) of leather, as seen on the Chertomlyk vase and at Sanchi in India. In the various Western countries horsemen were used to vaulting onto their horses' backs. However, in China the value

of the stirrup was already understood in the early 4th century (attested by the fig-
urine from Xiangshan, Nanjing). It facilitated not only ordinary riding, but also the
use of armor in cavalry warfare. The stirrup was first known in Europe in
Hungary in the 6th century AD, having presumably been brought there from
China by the steppe peoples. The saddle, however, was probably a development
that occurred throughout the Eurasian continent. Saddle and stirrup are two major
elements in riding astride and no doubt greatly advanced this practice.[42]

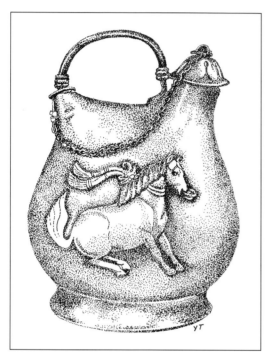

Figure 15

The Emperor's Dancing Horses

During the reign of Emperor Xuanzong (r. 712-756), a special troupe of 100 horses
was trained to perform for his amusement. The account of their performance and
their ultimate fate offers an insight into not only the high regard in which horses
were held by the Tang court, but also the special place that equines held in Chinese
mythology, especially in relationship to the dragon.

Xuanzong's Birthday Celebration - The "Thousand-Autumn Holiday," 729

In 729, Zhang Yuo, a minister to the court of Emperor Xuanzong, proposed that the
imperial birthday, the fifth day of the eighth lunar month, be declared a national
holiday. It would be called the "Thousand-Autumn Holiday" (*qian qiu jie*), to
express the wish for the Emperor's long life. Normal work and routines would be
suspended for three days during which celebrations in honor of the Emperor
would take place throughout the land. Xuanzong approved the request and
ordered that the inaugural Thousand-Autumn celebration take place that fall. This
initiated a tradition that would continue over the next two centuries.

These extravaganzas lasted throughout the night and included military presentations, dances, and various musical presentations. Elephants and rhinoceroses were
brought forth to the delight of the crowds. The highlight of the evening though
was invariably the performance of 100 specially trained "dancing horses." The
feats of these prancing equestrians not only delighted the crowd, but also provided
inspiration for the writers and poets of the court. In writing of the horses' performance, they sensed
and conveyed the strong link to ancient Chinese imagery and mythology.

Writings on the Dancing Horses

Zhang Yuo, while serving as collator for the imperial library, wrote the following description of
Xuanzong's dancing horses.

Hsüan Tsung [Xuanzong] once decreed that four hundred hooves be trained to
dance. [These hundred horses] were divided into companies of the Left and of the
Right, and styled "So-and-so Favorite" or "Such and-such Pride of the
Household." Occasionally there were also included excellent steeds that had been
sent as tribute from beyond the border. His Highness had them taught and trained,
and there was none but did not devote himself utterly to this wonderwork.

Thence, it was decreed that the horses be caparisoned with patterned embroidery,
haltered with gold and silver, and their manes and forelocks dressed out with
assorted pearls and jades. Their tune, which was called "Music for the Upturned
Cup," had several tens of choruses, to which they shook their heads and drummed
their tails, moving this way and that in response to the rhythm. Then wood-plank
platforms of three tiers were displayed. The horses were driven to the top of these,
where they turned and twirled round as if in flight. Sometimes it was ordered that
a doughty fellow lift one of the scaffolds, and the horse would [continue to] dance
atop it. There were a number of musicians who stood to the left and right, before

and behind; all were clothed in tunics of pale yellow, with patterned-jade belts, and all must be youths chosen for their handsome appearance and refined bearing. At every Thousand-Autumn Festival, beneath the Loft of Zealous Administration [the horses] danced by decree.

Subsequently, when His Highness graced Shu with his presence [fled Chang'an during the An Lushan rebellion], the dancing horses were for their part dispersed to the human world. An Lu-shan, having often witnessed their dancing, coveted them at heart; because of this he had several sold [to him] in Fan-yang. Subsequently, they were in turn acquired by T'ien Ch'eng-szu [Tian Chengsi]. He was ignorant of them [i.e., of their special talents]. Confusing them with steeds of battle, he installed them in the outer stables. Unexpectedly one day, when the soldiers of his army were enjoying a sacrificial feast and music was struck up, the horses, unable to stop themselves, began to dance. The servants and lackeys considered them bewitched and took brooms in hand to strike them. The horses thought that their dancing was out of step with the rhythm and, stooping and rearing, nodding and straining, they yet [tried to] realize their former choreography. The stablemaster hurried to report this grotesquerie, and Ch'eng-szu [Chengsi] ordered that the horses be flayed. The more fiercely this was done, the more precise became the horses' dancing. But the whipping and flogging ever increased, till finally they fell dead in their stalls. On this occasion there were in fact some persons who knew these were the [emperor's] dancing horses but, fearful of [Chengsi] wrath, they never ventured to speak.[43]

Song of the Upturned Cup

The horses performed to special music and lyrics known as the song of the "The Upturned Cup." Zhang Yuo, who had initially proposed the "Thousand-Autumn" festival, recorded the lyrics to six of the stanzas, three of which are shown below.

> The "myriad jewels" [courtiers] pay court at the levee of the phoenix screen;
> "Thousand-guilders" [sons of the wealthy] guide and lead the Dragon's Mediators.
> In promenade prancing, vigor concentrated, [the horses] glance aside at the drums,
> Pace to and fro in sportive shadows, paying heed to the song.

> With colorful tail-pennants the eight dancing rows form up into columns;
> The five hues of the temporal dragons [dragon-horses] are adapted to the directions.
> Bending their knees, they clench wine cups in mouth, attending to the rhythm;
> Inclining their hearts, they offer up longevity never ending.

> The dragon colts of the imperial fold are well-grouped, well composed;
> The thoroughbred foals from the astral corral are unwonted and uncommon.
> In easy expanse of gambade and prance, they answer to the rhythm,
> Full of high spirits, treading each other's prints, and never wavering.

Zhang Yuo also wrote three additional works in praise of the performance of the horses at the Thousand-Autumn festival.

> For the paragon born of the Heaven of Metal [Xuanzong] - a Holiday for One Thousand Autumns!
> The jade ale is shared, circulated - a toast for a myriad years of life!
> We have given ear to "The Purple Bayard," a song from the Archive of Music;
> [song referring to superior horses]
> How may it compare, though, with these prime steeds as they dance on their floriate mound?

> Curvetting in company, their conformation evokes transfigured dragons and fishes;
> In promenade prancing, their vigor concentrates a whole column of birds and beasts.

Year upon year, in accord with tradition, on the day one pointed to the tree,
[the Emperor's birthday]
Light and lightly, they come as companions, soaring on felicitous clouds.

In another poem, Zhang Yuo again describes the horses' dance to the music of "The Upturned Cup."

The Illustrious Paragon's [Xuanzong's] perfect virtue is equal to that of Heaven,
And Heavenly Horses come for this ceremony, from far west of the sea.
Sedately striding with pasterns flexed, now they bow down on both knees;
Though full of high mettle, they do not advance, but stamp with a thousand hooves.

Hispid whiskers and straining manes steadily sweep in time;
As drums grow riotous, the gambading bodies now rear abruptly upward!
And then to the end of the festal song they have wine cups clenched in their mouths,
And loll their heads and flicker their tails, getting drunk as mud!

In his third poem, Zhang Yuo evokes the imagery of mythical horses from past dynasties.

Afar it is rumored, our Illuminate, Sovereign loves unconventional talent;
And by jade whip and golden wings the 'Dragon's Mediators' have been led in.
If it not be accounted Battened White that now is here amongst us,
Surely that must be Flying Yellow come from above the sky!

Their silhouettes play with blossoms of sunlight, in mutual glimmer and shimmer;
Snorting breath frames cloudy hues, as they pace round to and fro.
Let it not be said that beneath the pylons peach flowers are dancing -
Instead, by the river, there are leaves of orchid now opening out!
[The last two lines refer to autumn.][44]

Earlier Instances of Dancing Horses

Tales of dancing horses were prevalent well before Xuanzong's troop performed at the Thousand-Autumn Festival. The earliest mention pertained to one of the horses brought back to Emperor Han Wudi from Ferghana, who was trained to bow and move in time with the cadence of the drums.

The first dancing troop is noted in 458 (Northern and Southern dynasties) when a group of performing horses was sent as a gift to the Song court in the north. Additional mention is made of performing horses at the Liang court in 505. While Emperor Xuanzong's were by far the most famous of the Tang dynasty's dancing horses, they were not the first. His uncle, Zhongzong, is said to have had a similar team during his brief rule (705-710).

The dancing horses performed for Xuanzong for a mere 27 years - from 729, the year of the first Thousand-Autumn Festival, to 756, when the An Lushan rebellion resulted in the dispersal of the horse troupe and the end of the most glorious age of the Tang. The dancing horses were a living symbol of the glory of Xuanzong's court and the grandeur of the Tang equestrian culture. While their likes would never again be seen at a Chinese royal court, memories of their magnificence would last throughout the imperial period.

Mythical Horses and Dragons

To fully comprehend the images created in Zhang Yuo's works requires a look to the origins and symbolism of some of the equine references contained within them, in particular "heavenly horses" and "dragon horses."

The "heavenly horses" alluded to in Tang descriptions of Xuanzong's steeds not only refer to the Han horses brought from Ferghana, but also to the mythical water born horse of the same period. While the water-born horse and the relationship of the horse to the dragon was discussed previously, its importance warrants further exploration.

In the *Lie Xian Zhuan* by Ma Shi Huang (Horse-Master Illustrious) it was noted that Ma, famous for his miraculous ability to cure horses, was also sought out by ailing dragons. This seems to indicate that the dragon, recognizing the kinship between himself and the horse, realized that Ma's special talents could also be of benefit to him. The indication here is that the horse and dragon possessed much in common, but worked their magic in different realms. This concept was well-stated by one of the most noted horsemen of the Han dynasty, General Ma Yuan, who once said; "For moving through the heavens, nothing compares with the dragon; for moving over the earth, nothing compares with the horse."[45] This fundamental attraction between the two creatures was obviously forged early in Chinese mythology.

Evidence of the continued belief in the powers of the dragon horse to bestow immortality upon its rider is shown in an account of the discovery of such a magical horse during the reign of Tang Emperor Xuanzong.

> In the twenty-seventh year of "Opened Prime" (i.e., 739 AD), Li Yung [Li Yong] (678-747) of Chiang-hsia [Jiangxia] was serving as Warden of Lin-tzu [Linzi]. In the autumn of this year he duly went into the mountains to gather the dusky and yellow stones [purported to extend ones life], when suddenly he happened upon an old gaffer. Quite wonderful in appearance, the old man's robust lineaments were hale and clear, and his moustaches and beard were exceptionally sleek. Of hodden were the clothes he wore. Emerging from off to the left of the road, he stayed Li Yung's [Li Yong's] horse and declared, "Surely you, my lord, are personally gathering medicaments that will serve to extend the years of our sagely ruler?" "It is so," said Yung [Yong]. "It were meet," [sic] said the gaffer, "if our sagely ruler procured a dragon-horse. In that case, he would for a myriad years enjoy the state and that without the trouble of gathering medicaments." "And where," said Yung [Yong], "might a dragon-horse be found?" "One may be expected on the moors of Ch'i [Qi] and Lu," replied the gaffer; "if it be procured, that would be a very talisman of greatest tranquility. Even unicorn, phoenix, tortoise, or dragon are not worthy to be paired with such a token." Yung [Yong] then ordered [the old man] to mount and ride behind him, but all at once the fellow vanished from sight.

> When the fifth month, in summer, of the twenty-ninth year of "Opened Prime" (741) arrived, Ch'ien-chen [Qianzhen] actually obtained the steed at the household of Ma Hui-en [Huien] of Pei-hai [Beihai] County, central Shantung [Shandong]. Its coloring was a mixed blue-black and white; its two flanks had fish-scale plating; its mane and tail were like the tufted bristles of a dragon; its whinnying call had truly the tone of a hollow flute; and in one day it could gallop three hundred li. When Ch'ien-chen [Qianzhen] inquired from whence it had come, Hui-en [Huien] said, "I had but a solitary mare. Upon bathing in the waters of the Tzu [Zi], she conceived and delivered. Accordingly, I called this horse by the name 'Dragonling' " [since it must have been sired by the resident dragon of the Zi River].

> Ch'ien-chen [Qianzhen] reported this immediately to Yung [Yong], who, quite delighted, memorialized the matter and presented the horse [to the sovereign]. His Highness was greatly pleased. He proclaimed that the Inner Stable should take especial care with the beast's food and fodder. And he commanded painters to depict its form, to be published and revealed both within [the court] and without.[46]

The An Lushan Rebellion and the Demise of the Tang

Control of military horses played a significant role in the rebellion of An Lushan which, although unsuccessful, decisively weakened the Tang dynasty. An Lushan, an able general of Turkish and

Sogdian ancestry, became a favorite of Emperor Xuanzong. Among the responsibilities given to him was extensive jurisdiction over the cavalry horses of the empire. Over time, An Lushan secretly selected the best warhorses and sent them to the territory under his personal control in the northeast, thus giving him a considerable advantage when he was ready to revolt and proclaim himself emperor in 755. An Lushan succeeded in capturing Chang'an in 756, and his rebellion was only quelled with the help of numerous foreign troops, including Moslems from far to the west.

While the Tang dynasty would continue until 907, after the An Lushan rebellion, it was never capable of reaching its former glory. From its founding in 618 until the rebellion, the Tang, for the first time in Chinese history, had established a domestic breeding program capable of meeting not only the majority of their horse needs, but also improving the quality of their stock based on external bloodstock. This must be regarded as the golden era of China's equestrian prowess.

After the disruption of the royal studs resulting from the rebellion, the Tang were never able to match this feat again. In the waning days of the dynasty, and on into the subsequent Song dynasty, horse shortages again became a chronic problem for the Chinese. This created a significant problem during the Song dynasty (960-1279), and eventually played a major role in the defeat of the Chinese at the hands of the Mongols, and the establishment of the first non-Chinese dynasty, the Yuan in 1279.

The Song Dynasty

With the fall of the Tang in 907, China was thrown into 53 years of chaos known as the Five dynasties period in the North and as the Ten Kingdoms era in the South. In 960 the mutinous officers of the Latter Zhou court staged a coup and installed a somewhat reluctant Zhao Kusngyin (Taizu) as its new emperor. Zhao, who had served as commander of the palace army, was able to reunify the country and establish the Song dynasty. A new capital was established in the northern city of Kaifeng.

China suffered from a weak military during the Song due in part to the demise of the concept of the citizen-soldier, so effectively used in past dynasties. These new professional soldiers were looked down on by a large segment of the population. Diplomacy replaced warfare in dealing with the hostile tribes to the north due in part to China's military inadequacies. In most other areas, however, the dynasty presided over China's renaissance. Art, technological innovation, philosophy, and literature flourished. With the development of wood block printing, wisdom from the past became accessible to a large segment of the population. The prosperity enjoyed during the Song allowed for the first time the development of a wealthy and educated middle class.

Horse Shortages

China's chronic shortage of horses for the military was quite severe throughout the Song dynasty. The problem was exacerbated by the fact that the Chinese were no longer able to recruit mercenary cavalry from the nomadic tribes as they had in the past. Song Qi, the famous scholar and, for a time superintendent of government pastures, noted:

> The reason why our enemies to the north and west are able to withstand China is precisely because they have many horses and their men are adept at riding; this is their strength. China has few horses, and its men are not accustomed to riding; this is China's weakness. . . The court constantly tries, with our weakness, to oppose our enemies' strength, so that we lose every battle. . . Those who propose remedies for this situation merely wish to increase our armed forces in order to overwhelm the enemy. They do not realize that, without horses, we can never create an effective military force.[47]

In a separate work, Song Qi also stated that, "while China had a large number of cavalrymen, only one or two out of ten had a horse to ride." As in the past, China's inability to maintain an adequate number of cavalry mounts placed them at a distinct disadvantage in dealing with their neighbors. This was not from lack of effort. Some of the leading officials of the time tried in vain to develop programs that would insure a constant supply of quality mounts. One of these attempted to establish a breeding ground in the rich farming area of the lower Yellow River Valley. While a noble attempt, pressure to use the land for more traditional agricultural purposes doomed the experiment to failure.[48]

For centuries, China had been trading silk for horses with its nomadic neighbors. The nature of these exchanges had varied since their inception determined by which of the trading partners was strongest at any particular time. During periods where nomadic strength equaled or exceeded that of China, it often became necessary for the Chinese to pay dearly in both barter items and gold for what in many cases were inferior horses. In 1077, the royal finance commissioner communicated to the Emperor that expenditures for military horses were one of the empire's greatest expenses.[49]

The demand for tea had increased greatly among the nomadic tribes by the Song dynasty. This in part coincided with the spread of Buddhism along the northern steppe. As a result, "Tea for Horses" markets were established along the border. As China controlled tea production, they attempted to maintain the price for tea at an artificially high level in order to acquire a greater number of horses from their neighbors.

Jurchen Invasion

Despite the best efforts of the Song, including frontier markets, diplomacy, and payment of tributes, mounted Jurchen warriors descended on China in 1127 and captured the Chinese capital of Kaifeng. The Song were forced to move their capital south to Hangzhou. With peace restored, Hangzhou developed into a thriving intellectual and cultural center and would remain so until the Mongol invasion more than a century later.[50] By 1275, it was the largest and richest city in the world.[51]

Descriptions of life in the teaming city alluded to rich men riding their horses through the streets and their wives being transported on chairs borne on the backs of men. Because the city was so crowded, most goods were transported on canals or by porters. When weight prohibited human portage, donkeys or mules were usually employed. A Japanese pilgrim who had visited Hangzhou in 1072 reported that the Chinese employed diminutive equines referred to as "rabbit horses" to move goods through the crowded city. These were purported to stand only 35 inches in height and to have ears measuring ten inches.[52] Unfortunately, little else about these horses is known.

The Yuan Dynasty
The Mongol Invasion

In 1162 an event occurred which would have a tremendous impact on not only China, but also on a large portion of the civilized world, the birth of Temujin, later known as Genghis Khan (1162-1227). At the time of his birth, the Mongols lacked unity, existing as a fragmented series of tribes. By 1203, Temujin, utilizing his genius for organization, had begun the process of unifying the various Mongol tribes into an effective and ruthless fighting force. Their horses and their riding tradition were their strengths. While the Mongols were never able to field massive armies, horses and their mastery of them, along with their unquestioning obedience to their leader, enabled them to conquer a major portion of the world.

The Mongols initially relied on the tough and hardy Mongolian horse. These horses generally stood between 13 and 14 hands and were in plentiful supply. An additional advantage of these horses was their ability to subsist solely on grass. This not only eliminated the costly expense of providing dietary supplements, but also provided the Mongols with the luxury of not having to carry this additional burden while on the march.

While the Mongols received great service from their native horses, this did not preclude attempts to improve their stock. When the Mongols took Beijing in 1251, one of their first acts was to expropriate the royal herds of the Chinese. While most of these horses were similar to the Mongols' own stock, the Chinese still processed remnants of the Ferghana "blood sweating" horses brought to China by Emperor Wudi during the Han dynasty. Eventually, these, and virtually all of China's superior breeding stock, would wind up in the hands of the invaders. The result was that when the Mongols were finally expelled, the quality of the horses of the Middle Kingdom had dropped substantially.

Figure 16

Mongol Horse Policy

The Mongols' ability to wage war was directly tied to their ability to maintain a supply of quality mounts. Extensive care was taken to insure that the supply remained in tack. While horses were "green broke" at an early age, they were not used in battle until they turned five. Great care was taken to insure that the horses submitted totally to their riders, an essential element on the field of battle. Military mounts consisted almost exclusively of geldings. This had the result of reducing problems with competing males while the army was on the march, and also insured that only superior stallions were allowed to breed.

The warhorses of the Mongols were trained to permit their riders to shoot a bow in all directions while at a gallop. The gallop was preferred as it provided a smoother shooting platform and because, at a gallop, a horse's head extends forward allowing the mounted archer a wider range of fire.

Mongol horsemen (Fig. 16) were divided into groups of 10, 100, and 1000. By leading extra horses as remounts, they could travel and fight up to 100 miles a day. In battle, much as in their great hunts on the steppe, tightly choreographed columns were used to encircle and compress the enemy. With these mobile tactics, the practice of deception, and the power of their heavy bows, which could kill at 600 feet, the Mongols brought offensive power to its height in the age before the full rise of firearms. Additionally, they were masters of espionage and psychological warfare, and showed a capacity to quickly absorb non-Mongol military techniques, most notably Chinese methods of city siege.

Once an army was on the march, Genghis Khan employed strict laws regarding the treatment and handling of horses.

> Take care of the led horses in your troop, before they lose condition. For once they have lost it, you may spare them as much as you will, they will never recover it on campaign.... You will encounter much game on the march. Do not let the men go after it ... do not let the men tie anything to the back of the saddle. Bridles will not be worn on the march - the horses are to have their mouths free. If this is done the men cannot march at a gallop. If an order has been given, then those who disobey it must be beaten and put under arrest. But as for those who have disobeyed my personal orders, send those who are worth serious consideration to me. The rest, the unimportant ones, are to be beheaded on the spot.[53]

As the army would near its objective, great care was given to provide the horses with sufficient rest prior to battle.

The Conquest of China

By 1215, Mongol troops had seized control of northern China and driven the Jurchen out of their capital, Yanjing (Beijing). After the death of Genghis in 1227, his empire was divided among his family. Toluli, his youngest son, was given control over much of Northern China, while his third son, Ogödei, became Khan of Khans, the empire's supreme ruler. After Ogödei's death, Toluli's son, Khubilai (1215-1294), became the supreme leader of all Mongol tribes.

The Mongols continued to expand and were poised along the border of the Southern Song by 1235. In 1276 Hangzhou fell, and by 1279 the Mongols were able to impose upon China the first alien dynasty in its history when Khubilai proclaimed the Yuan dynasty with himself as its emperor.

This was a humiliating period for the Chinese. The Mongols instituted a four-class system with the Mongols at the top. They had complete control of the military, particularly the cavalry. Native Chinese were only allowed to serve in the infantry. The Mongols were followed in importance and influence by immigrants from Turkestan and Europe, Northern Chinese including the Khitans and Manchurians, with the Chinese remnants of Southern Song dynasty at the bottom of the heap. This group was even forbidden from riding horses.

With the safety of travel afforded by the vast territory under the control of the Mongols, and their fascination with and openness to western contact, exchanges between Europe and China became much more common. One of the more famous Europeans to venture to China was the Italian, Marco Polo, who spent 17 years as an adviser to the Great Khan.

The Horses of Khubilai Khan

When Marco Polo returned to Italy and recorded his experiences in China, many of his references pertained to horses. Among others, he described how the Great Khan maintained a band of 10,000 snow-white mares that provided milk for the royal palace. Each year, the Emperor would leave his palace for an inspection tour of the herd.

Marco Polo described in great detail the Khan's royal messenger service, which could bring information from every corner of his vast empire within a matter of days. The service consisted of more than 10,000 posts stationed every 40 to 48 kilometers along all major roads. All were supplied with luxurious rest houses and a complement of 400 horses provided by the local population as part of the taxation system. 200 were turned out to graze, while the other 200 were held ready to be taken on to the next post by messengers. Messengers approaching the stations would use a bell to announce their arrival so that the rider for the next stage of the route could be prepared to immediately proceed. Using this system, it was said that riders could cover 250 miles per day.

Horse Breeding during the Yuan Dynasty

It would be logical to think that, given the Mongols' expertise in horse breeding, this would have carried over to China during their occupation. Regarding the native Chinese horse population, what systematic breeding programs that had been in place soon disintegrated, with horses left to breed freely without concern for quality. This seems, however, not to have been the case.

> The Chinese do not seem to have gone in much for horse breeding since the Mongol conquest, depending for their supplies of these animals upon Mongolia. China is the chief market for gelded Mongol ponies of from four to eight years. The Mongols seem disinclined to part with their mares, requiring them for breeding purposes. Such mares as do happen to reach China are usually crossed with donkeys to produce mules, which are considered superior to horses, both as draft and pack animals.[54]

As for the Mongols themselves, Morris Rossabi describes the Great Khan's measures to insure a steady supply of mounts.

> Khubilai also recognized the military value of horses and knew that a sensible system of obtaining horses was needed. Now that some Mongols were settling in the sedentary world, they began to face the same problems as the Chinese in acquiring

horses. For the expansion of his domain and for defense against his enemies, Khubilai had to have a dependable supply of horses suitable for warfare. Therefore, Khubilai fashioned a "horse administration" and devised regulations guaranteed to protect his steeds. He established the Court of the Imperial Stud to tend his own herds as well as to manage horses assigned to the postal stations and to the imperial guards and armies. Under the regulations issued by his court, one out of every one hundred horses owned by the people was to be turned over to the government. Khubilai also reserved the right to purchase horses, and owners were compelled to sell their animals at official prices. On occasion, he even requisitioned horses without compensating their owners, and offered the following justification: "Horses have already been requisitioned from those Buddhist monks, Christians, Taoists, Mohammedan teachers of North China who had them.... Now what need have the monks and Taoists, sitting in their temples, of horses?" There were severe punishments for Chinese families who concealed their horses, as there were for Chinese or Muslim merchants who smuggled them across the border to be sold to Khubilai's enemies. Mongol control over such smuggling was, to Khubilai, essential.[55]

The Ming Dynasty

After the death of Khubilai Khan in 1294, the Yuan court experienced a succession of mediocre rulers. This, combined with continued Chinese resentment of the Mongols and a series of natural disasters, made the dynasty ripe for overthrow. Secret Chinese societies became increasingly powerful. In 1356 Zhu Yuanzhang, a former monk turned rebel leader, and his peasant army captured the southern capital of Nanjing. Within a decade he had won control of the economically important middle and lower reaches of the Yangtze River, driving the Mongols to the north. In 1368 he proclaimed the Ming dynasty (1368-1644) with himself as Emperor. Zhu chose the name Hongwu for his reign and established his capital at Nanjing on the lower Yangtze. Later the same year he captured the Yuan capital of Beijing. By 1367, the Mongols had been driven from China. In 1402, Zhu's successor, the Yongle emperor began building a new seat of power on the site of the old Yuan capital in Beijing.

Under the Yongle emperor, China developed into a major maritime power. Zheng He, a eunuch general of Muslim descent, undertook seven great expeditions that took him and a huge fleet to Southeast Asia, Persia, Arabia and eastern Africa.

Horses in the Ming Dynasty

China once again faced the critical problem of securing horses at the onset of the Ming dynasty. This was exacerbated by the fact that the Mongols had depleted China of most of its quality breeding stock during the Yuan. With raids from the north still a problem, the Ming were forced to import more than 10,000 horses per year during its first century, and nearly that many throughout the life of the dynasty.

The "tea for horses" markets originally established during the Song, were reinvigorated. The Ming Court strictly controlled the price of tea in an effort to create a more favorable rate in the trade for horses. As a result, from 1404 to 1423, the Ming were able to increase their horse population from 50,000 to around 1,600,000 through trade and tribute. During both the Ming and Qing dynasties, a significant effort was made to import superior horses to increase the size and strength of China's military stock.[56] This, however, met with only modest success.

Although the Chinese had invented gunpowder around 1040, they never really seemed to seize its military potential, particularly in regards to their cavalry. During the late Ming dynasty it was noted that the cavalryman still relied on the bow as his primary weapon. This preference for the bow over firearms would continue into the Qing dynasty and was not necessarily a liability. In many ways loading and firing a bow from horseback was superior to trying to wield and reload the bulky and often inaccurate rifles of the time.

Towards the end of the Ming dynasty, the Manchus were gaining in strength to the north and increasingly were crossing into China seeking plunder. On one such raid into Hebei and Shandong, they were able to escape with more than 550,000 horses and cattle. Initially, however, it was not the Manchus who would bring the Ming dynasty to an end.

In the final years of Ming rule, official corruption, excessive eunuch power, intellectual conservatism, and costly wars in Korea and ultimately China itself, brought the nation to the brink of bankruptcy. A famine in Shaanxi Province and governmental neglect sparked a huge peasant rebellion. In 1644 a rebel leader was able to gain access to the capital prompting the last Ming emperor to commit suicide. In an attempt to restore order, the Chinese sought the help of the Manchus. Once they quelled the rebellion, however, the Manchus refused to leave, and in 1644 proclaimed the Qing dynasty (1644-1912).

The Qing Dynasty

The Manchus, like the Mongols, had a long tradition of equestrian excellence. It is important to note, however, that the Manchus did not share the Mongol heritage of nomadic pastoralism. As Pamela Crossley points out, "the Qing Empire led by the Manchus was not nomadic in economic impulsion, in political organization, or in style."[57] In fact, until the Khitans dominated Manchuria in the tenth century, very few horses existed there, and the local population subsisted primarily on hunting, fishing, and gathering. Once exposed to neighboring horse cultures, the Manchus soon mastered the arts of horsemanship and of horseback archery, and were accomplished equestrians by the time of the Qing.

In viewing the Qing, all too often we tend to look at its waning years while failing to give full credit to its earlier accomplishments. The fact is that the Qing was able to create one of the greatest empires of its day, a rival to both the Turkish Ottoman and the Russian Romanov (Romanoff) empires. Even after expansion that resulted in the largest contiguous land-based empire in the world, the Qing maintained an effective fighting force that was not only able to control its vast empire, but also to thwart Russian efforts to expand towards the Pacific.

While little is known of the personal lives of most of China's imperial rulers, the Kangxi Emperor (r. 1661 - 1722) is an exception. Throughout his reign, he was known for his candor, and many of his private thoughts and feelings have survived. As a child, Kangxi had been well trained in the traditional Manchu martial and equestrian skills. The emperor was quite at home on the back of a horse. He frequently traveled his empire on inspection tours, meeting officials and allowing his subjects to see their grand emperor. In military affairs, the emperor personally led his armies into battle on several occasions.

Kangxi seemed to have a great affinity for the hunt. While ceremonial royal hunts had been popular since the Shang dynasty, the hunts of the Kangxi emperor were far from ceremonial. These were the more vigorous Manchu-type hunts, often taking place north of the Great Wall. The emperor was known to use these occasions as an opportunity to train and evaluate his troops, sometimes taking up to 2,000 soldiers on a single trip. He realized that no cavalryman could be skilled at archery unless he was also skilled at riding, and saw the hunt as an opportunity to hone both of these skills.

Prior to setting out with his entourage, the emperor would have shamans offer a traditional Manchu blessing for the horses.

> Oh Lord of Heaven, Oh Mongol leaders, Manchu princes, we pray to you for our swift horse. Through your power may their legs lift high, their manes toss; may they swallow the winds as they race, and grow ever sleeker as they drink in the mists, may they have fodder to eat, and be healthy and strong; may they have roots to nibble, and reach a great age. Guard them from ditches, front the

precipices over which they might fall; keep them far from thieves. Oh gods, guard them; Oh spirits, help them![58]

For more than a century and a half the Qing cavalry served as a well organized and efficient force that helped to expand the empire and protect against foreign encroachments along China's borders.

However, after an extended period of peace, decadence and corruption had spread throughout the imperial court by the beginning of the nineteenth century. There was subsequently a decline of the Manchu military spirit, which was reflected in the increasing inefficiency of the Qing cavalry.

With the foreign incursions and gunboat diplomacy of the nineteenth century, the cavalry of the Manchus proved no match for the superior firepower and landmines of the Europeans and Americans. This was not solely a Chinese phenomenon, but one that would be played out many times on a world stage. The culmination would come in Europe during World War I when the horse cavalry would cease to exist as a major force in modern warfare.

Conclusion

In looking at the equestrian history of China, it is necessary to keep in mind that geographically, China's borders were incredibly elastic throughout the dynastic period, sometimes exceeding but often encompassing much less territory than the borders of the modern People's Republic. As such, there were long periods when the western and northern regions, with their rich pasturelands and strong equestrian traditions, were not included in China proper. China's heart was always agrarian in nature. This was mandated by its need to feed its citizenry, a critically central element in the covenant between the emperor and his subjects. As the ox was the preferred draft animal in this region, the horse never became an intrinsic part of mainstream Chinese culture.

Throughout a large portion of its imperial history, China was the most advanced and sophisticated society in the world. This was certainly the case at the time that the Chinese were forced to develop an effective cavalry in order to defend its northern and western borders. The fact that riding was an importation from what were considered barbarian cultures, did not fit well with the xenophobic assumption that all things of value emanated from the Middle Kingdom. Exclusive of the two dynasties initiated and controlled by foreign elements, the few brief intervals when equestrian appreciation and accomplishment were at their zenith invariably coincided with the periods when China was controlled by peoples native to their northern or western pastoral regions.

Throughout the imperial period, China's inability to develop a consistent internal breeding program to meet its military needs cost it dearly both economically and geographically. Barring raising their own stock, the Chinese were left with only three options to secure the horses it so desperately needed - tribute, plunder, and purchase. While the first two options did supply some of the needed steeds, purchase remained the only reliable way for the Chinese to supply their military with essential mounts. Economically, during a majority of the dynasties, China was forced to expend a large portion of her wealth to secure horses from external sources. Geographically, the nomadic horsemen of the steppe were often able to seize and control vast areas along her borders based on their equestrian superiority.

It is a credit to the ingenuity of the Chinese, however, that despite the fact that the horse never fully was integrated into their culture, they still were able to provide three of history's most important equestrian inventions; the stirrup, the breast-strap harnessing system, and the horse collar. Also to their credit is the vast legacy of equestrian related artistic and cultural relics which we value and respect so much today.

In modern China the horse continues to play a significant role not only in its historical and mythological soul, but also in the daily life of many of her citizens, particularly those in the western and northern provinces. China now has the largest equine population in its history, with more than 26 distinct breeds within its borders. It seems safe to assume that as the Chinese economic progress of the last 20 years continues, the horse will continue to play an important utilitarian and increasingly recreational role in her development.

Qin Shi Huang's Terracotta Army

Bill Cooke

In 247 BC, Prince Zheng assumed control of the State of Qin. Within ten years, he led his armies to the defeat of the six competing states and united China for the first time. After unification, Cheng assumed the name of Qin Shi Huang, "first august emperor." He consolidated his power by stabilizing the northern border and pacifying the various tribes in the south, and established China's first empire, with centralized power held in his hands and those of his advisors. Qin Shi Huang succeeded in unifying statutes, weights and measures, currency, and written script throughout his empire. He built more than 4,000 miles of imperial highways, and 1,200 miles of canals. China's first emperor, however, was a tyrannical ruler whose severe laws, heavy taxation, and ceaseless military campaigns created great hardship for his subjects.

Qin Shi Huang was obsessive in his quest for immortality. In an attempt to learn the secrets of the legendary "immortals," he made numerous pilgrimages to sacred mountains throughout his empire. He also was in a constant search for elixirs that might prolong his life. One of these efforts, the ingestion of mercury, is suspected to have led to his death at age 50.

The 1974 discovery of the terracotta army at Qin Shi Huang's necropolis near Lintong, 35 kilometers from the city of Xi'an in Shaanxi Province, was one of the most significant archaeological finds of the century. Beginning in the Eastern Zhou dynasty, miniature pottery figures representing people, animals, and other aspects from life were often buried with the dead. The more important the deceased, the more elaborate and numerous the items interred with them. This seems to have been a more practical substitution for entombing actual people, horses, and other livestock that had been prevalent in previous periods. This is not to say that human and animal sacrifice was no longer present in Qin burials. The first emperor's necropolis also contained the remains of many equine and human victims. Notable are the royal stables located just east of the terracotta army. These pits contain the remains of hundreds of horses attended by kneeling terracotta stable boys or grooms. However, the terracotta figures, of which the army is comprised, represent the first time in China that large quantities of life-size replicas were used as tomb figures.

The terracotta army represents but one part of the massive necropolis complex that is dominated by the large, central tumulus covering the still unexcavated tomb of the Emperor. The imperial necropolis was under construction from 246 BC until Qin Shi Huang's death in 210 BC. *The Historical Records (Shiji) of Sima Qian* describe the construction of the royal tomb and the burial of the Emperor.

> When the First Emperor had just come the throne, excavations and building work had taken place at Mount Li, but when he unified all under Heaven, convicts the number of more than 700,000 were sent there from all over the Empire. They dug through three springs and poured down molten bronze to make the outer coffin; and replicas of palaces, pavilions, all the various officials, and wonderful vessels and other rare objects were brought up to the tomb, which was then filled with them. Craftsmen were ordered to make crossbows and arrows which would operate automatically so that anyone who approached what had been excavated was immediately shot. Quicksilver was used to represent the various waterways, the Yangtze and Yellow Rivers, and the great sea, being made by some mechanism to flow into each other, and above were ranged the heavenly constellations and below was the layout of the land. Candles were made of whale fat, for it was reckoned that it would be a long time before they were extinguished.
>
> Second Generation [Qin Shi Huang's son, Emperor Er Shi] said: 'It would not be right that any of the previous Emperor's concubines should emerge from this place unless she has a son.' They were all ordered to accompany him in death, and those who died were extremely numerous. After the burial had taken place someone mentioned the fact that the workers and craftsmen who had constructed the mechanical devices would know about all the buried treasures and the importance of the treasures would immediately be disclosed. Consequently when the great occasion was finished and after the treasures had been hidden away, the main entrance-way to the tomb was shut off, and the outer gate lowered, so that all the workers and craftsmen who had buried the treasure were shut in, and there were none who came out again. And vegetation and trees were planted to make it look like a hill.[59]

The burial pits containing the terracotta army lie approximately one and one-quarter kilometer east of the royal tomb. To date, five pits have been discovered relating to the army. This includes the most recent discovery, a pit containing a vast quantity of stone armor discovered in October 1999. Pit number one, discovered in 1974, is the largest, containing more than 6,000 soldiers and horses, along with several chariots. This is thought to represent the right, or main, army. In 1976, a second pit was discovered which, along with 1,400 terracotta soldiers, cavalrymen, and horses, contained 90 wooden war chariots. In 1980, what is thought to be the army's command center was discovered containing one chariot, four horses, and 68 soldiers. The same year, two magnificent bronze vehicles, each drawn by four bronze horses, were discovered in a separate sacrificial pit parallel to the terracotta army. One additional pit was also found, however, no figures or artifacts were present. Some speculate that this may have represented a work in progress at the time of the Emperor's death. In total, more than 7,000 figures, 600 horses, and tens of thousands of bronze spears and arrows have been found along with a great array of other objects.

Pits one and two were constructed as a series of parallel trenches with earthen walls supported by wooden columns. The roof beams spanning the trenches were covered with straw and bamboo mats. Impressions of the mats are still visible on some of the earthen divisions within the tomb. Pit three is much smaller than one and two.

Most of the terracotta soldiers, horses, and other material found in the tomb had suffered extensive damage. This probably occurred when the roof collapsed following the burning of the necropolis. It is believed that the blaze was started by the rebel Xiang Yu after his overthrow of Er Shi, Qin Shi Huang's son and successor. Sources indicate that this fire may have burned for up to three months.

The uniforms of Qin Shi Huang's army varied by rank and duty, and may be roughly divided into the dress of officers and regular soldiers.

There are three grades of officers shown in the terracotta army: senior, intermediate, and junior. The senior officers are represented by the seven figures, which have usually been referred to as generals, but in fact represent officers of the eighth rank within the 20-rank Qin system. Their dress was characterized by double tunics covered by painted "fish-scale" armor. They wore long trousers and shoes with square, up-thrusting toes. The higher-ranking officers wore "he" caps, named for a tenacious type of pheasant known to fight to the death when provoked.

The uniforms of the intermediate officers were characterized by their armor of overlapping square plates that extended to below the waist, and provided protection for the shoulders and upper arms. The original armor was constructed of lacquered leather. Under the armor, a tunic extended to below the knees. The middle officers wore a double-boarded cap and squared shoes with upturned toes.

The junior officers wore a tunic covered by a breastplate, a single-boarded cap, puttees (a strip of cloth wound spirally around the leg from the ankle to the knee), and low-cut shoes or short boots.

Soldiers' Dress

The figures of light infantrymen were clothed in belted tunics, knee breeches, leggings and low-cut shoes. Their hair was gathered into a bun and fastened on top-right side of the head.

The uniforms of the heavy infantrymen consisted of armor-covered tunics, knee breeches, puttees, low-cut shoes or short boots with the hair tied in a round bun or covered by a skullcap. In some cases they also wore shinguards.

The chariot-borne warriors or guards wore uniforms similar to those of the heavy-infantry. The chariot drivers wore either: (1) a breastplate (but no gauntlet) over a long robe, shin guards, low-cut shoes and officers cap; or (2) a complete suit of armor including a gorget (a piece of armor protecting the throat), and brassards (a cloth badge worn around the upper arm) and gauntlets which cover the arms and extended over the wrists and hands.

The cavalrymen were dressed in the style reflecting that of the nomadic horsemen living on the country's northern and western borders. They wore short breastplates reaching down to the waist, long trousers, short boots, and skullcaps.

All of the terracotta army figures were made using local clay, which was first sifted, washed, and combined with ground quartz. The base and feet were molded with the legs. The torso was constructed using coiled strips of clay, and the separately molded arms were attached to the torso. The head and hands were then roughcast in composite molds, and after the addition of the nose, ears, and hair, both the head and hands were given individual characteristics.

The horses were first roughcast, with additional clay applied and carved to create the details. The head was cast in two parts, with hand-molded ears and elements such as saddles and bridles added later. The horse's muzzle was hand modeled, then attached to the head. Because of the horse's weight, the legs were tempered for extra strength. The neck and trunk were formed from molds and then joined. All of the horses had a small hole in the side of the torso to release the pressure which would build up during firing. Lute, a smooth, paste-like clay, was used to attach extraneous elements such as ears and tails.

The figures were fired at approximately 1,000 degrees Celsius (1,832 degrees Fahrenheit), and then painted with pigments suspended in a lacquer base. The principle colors used were vermilion, claret, pink, greens, purple, blues, azure, yellow, orange, white and ochre.

Endnotes

1   Sun Ji, personal interview, Beijing, 17 March 1999.

2   Sandra Olsen, ed., *Horses through Time*, (Boulder, Colo.: Robert Rienhart Publisher for Carnegie Museum of Natural History, no date) 95.

3   Bonnie Hendricks, *International Encyclopedia of Horse Breeds*, (Norman, Okla.: University of Oklahoma Press, 1995) 123.

4   Olsen 63.

5   H. G. Creel. "The Role of the Horse in Chinese History." *American Historical Review* 70, no. 3 (April 1965): 653.

6   Creel 656.

7   Jenny F. So and Emma C. Bunker, *Traders and Raiders on China's Northern Frontier*, (Seattle: Arthur M. Sackler Gallery, Smithsonian Institute in association with the University of Washington Press, 1995) 26.

8   Arthur Waley, *Translations from the Chinese*, (New York: Alfred A. Knopf, 1941) 14.

9   Chen Quanfan, et al., *Xi'an: Legacies of Ancient Chinese Civilization*, (Beijing: Morning Glory Press, 1992), 93-95.

10 Michael Loewe, *Everyday Life in Early Imperial China During the Han Period 202 BC AD 220*, (New York: Dorset Press, 1968) 140-141.

11 Joseph Needham, *Science and Civilisation in China, vol. 4, Physics and Physical Technology, part 2: Mechanical Engineering*, (Cambridge, England: Cambridge University Press, 1965) 304.

12 Needham 207-208.

13 Needham 313.

14 Robert Temple, *The Genius of China; 3,000 Years of Science, Discovery, and Invention*, (United Kingdom: Multimedia Publications, 1986) 22-23.

15 Creel 655.

16 D. C. Lau and Roger T. Ames, *Sun Pin: The Art of Warfare*, (New York: Ballantine Books, 1996), 44-45

17 Lau and Ames 48.

18 Lau and Ames 259.

19 Albert Dien, "The Stirrup and Its Effect on Chinese Military History," *Ars Orientalis* 16 (1986): 33-36.

20 Yang Hong, "Weapons of Ancient China," (Beijing: Science Press, 1992), 239, 240, 244.

21 Chen 93.

22 Dien 37-38.

23 Creel 657.

24 Jonathan Maslow, "The Golden Horses of Turkmenistan", *Aramco World* 48, no. 5 (May-June 1997), 15 November 1999 <http://www.silk-road.com/>.

25 Creel 661.

26 Robert E. Harrist, Jr., *Power and Virtue: The Horse in Chinese Art*, (New York: China Institute in America, 1997) 54.

27 Barbara Chapman Banks, "The Magical Powers of the Horse as Revealed in Archeological Explorations of Early China," Ph. D. diss., University of Chicago, 1989, 214.

28 Arthur Waley, "The Heavenly Horses of Ferghana: A New View," *History Today* (February 1955): 96-97.

29 Waley, "Heavenly Horses" 97-98.

30 Creel 658.

31 Creel 658.

32 Creel 665.

33 Loewe 160-161.

34 Banks 242-245.

35 Creel 666.

36 Ann Paludan, *Chronicle of the Chinese Emperors*, (London: Thames and Hudson, 1998) 94-95

37 Paul Kroll, "The Dancing Horses of the Tang," *T'oung Pao* LXVII, no. 3-5 (1981): 264.

38 Jacques Gernet, *A History of Chinese Civilization*, 2d ed. (Cambridge, England: Cambridge University Press, 1996; reprint 1999) 247-250.

39 Virginia L. Bower, "Polo in Tang China: Sport and Art," *Asian Art* (winter 1991): 27,32.

40 Harrist 74.

41 "Polo," Silk Road Foundation, 1997, 15 November 1999 <http://www.silk-road.com/games.shtml.>

42 Sun Ji, "The Equestrian Gear and Ornament of the Tang Dynasty," *Wenwu* 10 (1981): 82-88, 96.

43 Kroll 244-246.

44 Kroll 266-268.

45 Kroll 253-254.

46 Kroll 253-254

47 Creel 667.

48 Gernet, *A History of Chinese Civilization* 310.

49 Creel 667.

50 Patricia Ebrey, ed., *Chinese Civilization: A Sourcebook*, (New York: Free Press, 1991) 138.

51 Jacques Gernet, *Daily life in China on the Eve of the Mongol Invasion 1250-1276*, trans. H. M. Wright (Stanford: Stanford University Press, 1962) 14.

52 Gernet, *Daily Life in China...* 41.

53 Ann Hyland, *The Medieval Warhorse: From Byzantium to the Crusades*, (London: Grange Books, 1994) 135.

54 Creel 668.

55 Morris Rossabi, *Khubilai Khan, His Life and Times*, (Berkley: University of California Press, 1988) 129.

56 H. Epstein, *Domestic Animals in China*, US edition. (New York: Africana Publishing Corp., 1971) 98.

57 Pamela Kyle Crossley, *The Manchus*, (Cambridge, Mass.: Blackwell Publishers, 1997) 3.

58 Jonathon D. Spence, *Emperor of China, Self-portrait of K'ang-hsi*, (New York; Vintage Books, 1988) 12.

59 Raymond Dawson (translator), Sima Qian, Historical Records (Shiji), (Oxford University Press, Oxford, England, 1994, 85,86

Artifacts

Imperial China:
The Art of the Horse in Chinese History

馬

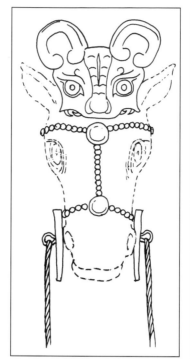

Figure 1

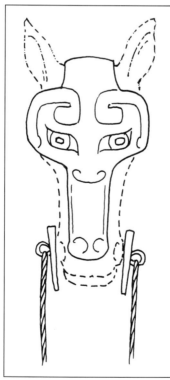

Figure 2

1

Tiger Horse Face Mask

Bronze; h. 15.5 cm, w. 19.8 cm
Western Zhou Dynasty (ca. 1100-771 BC)
Excavated in 1976 at Zhuyuangou in Baoji City,
Shaanxi Province.
Weibin District Museum of Baoji City

2

Horse Face Mask

Bronze; h. 39 cm, w. 21.9 cm
Western Zhou Dynasty (ca. 1100-771 BC)
Excavated in 1976 at Zhuyuangou in Baoji City,
Shaanxi Province.
Weibin District Museum of Baoji City

During the Western Zhou dynasty chariot harness was richly ornamented. This sometimes included a frontlet at the center of the horse's face, and bronze ornaments forming a mask on the eyes and nose. A further mask was often mounted above the ears. (Fig. 1) Bronze masks of this type from the Western Zhou dynasty are rarely found.

3

Two Tiger Head, Harness Decorations

Bronze; h. 3.9 cm
Western Zhou Dynasty (ca. 1100-771 BC)
Excavated in 1980 at Huangdui Town in Fufeng County,
Shaanxi Province.
Shaanxi Zhouyuan Museum

4

Openwork Harness Decorations

Bronze; h. 6.5 cm
Western Zhou Dynasty (ca. 1100-771 BC)
Excavated in 1980 at Huangdui Town in Fufeng County,
Shaanxi Province.
Shaanxi Zhouyuan Museum

5

Female Dancing Figure

Bronze; h. 11.6 cm
Western Zhou Dynasty (ca. 1100-771 BC)
Excavated in 1974 at Rujiazhuang Village in Baoji City,
Shaanxi Province.
Baoji Municipal Museum

In China's slave society those with talent were sometimes exempted from heavy labor and were trained to
sing and dance for the Imperial court and the nobility.
This practice began during the Xia and Shang dynasties
and continued through the Western Zhou. While the
exact usage of these pieces is unknown, both have
square holes at their bases, which would have allowed
them to be attached to wooden rods.

Figure 3

6

Male Dancing Figure

Bronze; h. 17.9 cm
Western Zhou Dynasty (ca. 1100-771 BC)
Excavated in 1974 at Rujiazhuang Village in Baoji City,
Shaanxi Province.
Baoji Municipal Museum

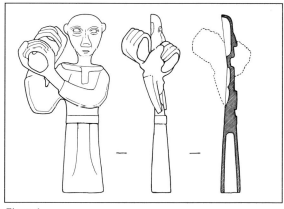

Figure 4

7

Arc-shaped Jingle

Bronze; l. 30 cm
Western Zhou Dynasty (ca. 1100-771 BC)
Excavated in 1980 at Zhuyuangou of Baoji City,
Shaanxi Province.
Shaanxi Baoji Municipal Museum

Jingles were frequently found with buried chariots and their associated weapons, and were once thought to be ornamentation for chariots. While the exact use of these objects is still debated, most feel that they belong with the weapons rather than with the vehicles. They may have been part of a composite bow carried by a warrior in a chariot, (Fig. 5) or an ornament of some other item of equipment. The composite bow, characteristic of eastern Asia, is constructed in three parts, of which the outer two parts are bent back in use. The jingle is thought by some scholars to be part of the mechanism for straightening the bow. This piece features a cicada design on a cloud background.

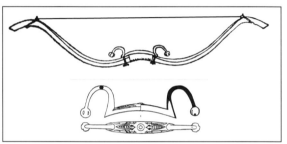

Figure 5

8

Chariot Pole End-Cap

Bronze; l. 7 cm, d. 3.3 cm
Western Zhou Dynasty (ca. 1100-771 BC)
Found in Fengxiang County in Shaanxi Province.
Shaanxi Fengxiang County Museum

9

Decorative Protective Cover for Front Wooden Bar of a Chariot

Bronze; l. 20.4 cm, d. 3.2 cm
Western Zhou Dynasty (ca. 1100-771 BC)
Excavated at Zhouyuan in Qishan County, in
Shaanxi Province.
Zhouyuan Museum of Qishan County

During the Western Zhou dynasty, chariots were essential military elements. Their role, however, may well have been more as a mobile command post or as a status symbol for their owners. Chariots, lacking an adequate suspension system, were only effective militarily when deployed on flat and solid ground.

CHARIOT DECORATIONS

10

Tiger-Shaped Chariot Ornaments

Bronze; h. 6.2 cm, l. 10.4 cm
Western Zhou Dynasty (ca. 1100-771 BC)
Excavated at Huangdui Town in Fufeng County,
Shaanxi Province.
Shaanxi Zhouyuan Museum

11

Dragon-Shaped Chariot Ornaments

Bronze; l. 13.2 cm
Western Zhou Dynasty (ca. 1100-771 BC)
Unearthed in 1980 at Zhuangou in Baoji City,
Shaanxi Province.
Shaanxi Baoji Municipal Museum

12

Prone Tiger Chariot Ornament

Bronze; h. 6 cm, l. 9.5 cm
Western Zhou Dynasty (ca. 1100-771 BC)
Excavated at Huangdui Town in Fufeng,
Shaanxi Province.
Shaanxi Zhouyuan Museum

13

Crawling Tiger Harness Ornament

Bronze; h. 12.4 cm, l. 26.4 cm
Western Zhou Dynasty (ca. 1100-771 BC)
Unearthed in 1980 at Zhuangou in Baoji City,
Shaanxi Province.
Shaanxi Baoji Municipal Museum

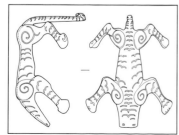

Figure 6

Chariot pole ornaments were made of bronze and are usually cylindrical in shape with one end open. This would have been slipped over the end of the pole and held into place with a bronze pin. There are holes in the base of each ornament to secure them to the pole.

14
Four Petal Chariot Pole End-Cap
Bronze; h. 7 cm, d. 3.8 cm
Western Zhou Dynasty (ca. 1100-771 BC)
Excavated at Qijia Village in Fufeng County,
Shaanxi Province.
Shaanxi Zhouyuan Museum

15
Two Hat-Like Chariot Pole End-Cap
Bronze; h. 12.5 cm, d. 4.8 cm
Western Zhou Dynasty (ca. 1100-771 BC)
Found in 1980 at Zhuyuangou in Baoji City,
Shaanxi Province.
Shaanxi Baoji Municipal Museum

Each of the hat-shaped decorations has an animal face in relief on the front. At the back of each, there is a figure that appears to be holding the animal face in both arms. (Fig. 7)

16
Animal Head Chariot Pole End-Cap
Bronze; h. 9.6 cm, d. 6.6 cm
Western Zhou Dynasty (ca. 1100-771 BC)
Found in 1980 at Zhuyuangou in Baoji City,
Shaanxi Province.
Shaanxi Baoji Municipal Museum

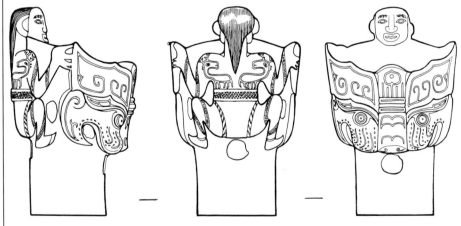

Figure 7

17

Two Shield-Shaped Chariot Ornaments

Bronze; h. 11.4 cm, w. 7.55 cm
Western Zhou Dynasty (ca. 1100-771 BC)
Excavated at Qiangjia Village in Fufeng County,
Shaanxi Province.
Shaanxi Provincial Zhouyuan Museum

18

Tiger and Ox Face Harness Ornaments

Bronze; h. 6.5 cm, w. 4.7 cm
Western Zhou Dynasty (ca. 1100-771 BC)
Discovered in 1980 at Zhuyuangou in Baoji City,
Shaanxi Province.
Shaanxi Baoji Museum

The rectangular animal head ornaments are identical in shape and size; one has a tiger's face and the other an oxen. At the back of each are bars for attachment to the harness of the horse.

19

Animal Face Harness Ornament

Bronze; h. 6 cm, w. 6.8 cm
Western Zhou Dynasty (ca. 1100-771 BC)
Discovered in 1980 at Zhuyuangou in Baoji City,
Shaanxi Province.
Shaanxi Baoji Museum

20

Ox-Head with Birds Harness Ornament

Bronze; h. 5.8 cm, w. 3.7 cm
Western Zhou Dynasty (ca. 1100-771 BC)
Discovered in 1980 at Zhuyuangou in Baoji City,
Shaanxi Province.
Shaanxi Baoji Museum

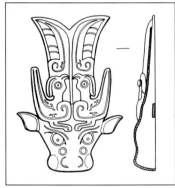

21

Ox with Two Birds Forming Horns, Chariot Harness Ornament

Bronze; h. 21.1 cm
Western Zhou Dynasty (ca. 1100-771 BC)
Discovered in 1980 at Zhuyuangou in Baoji City,
Shaanxi Province.
Shaanxi Baoji Museum

The animal-bird ornament is designed with an ox head surmounted by two birds with raised crests which form the horns of the ox. (Fig. 8)

Figure 8

22

Eyed-Shaped Chariot Harness Ornament

Bronze; h. 6 cm, w. 9 cm
Western Zhou Dynasty (ca. 1100-771 BC)
Excavated at Qiangjia Village in Fufeng County,
Shaanxi Province.
Shaanxi Provincial Zhouyuan Museum

Figure 9

These axle covers fit between the body of the chariot and the wheel. The rectangular plates were provided to scrape away mud from the chariot wheels.

23

Inner Chariot Axle Cover

Bronze; l. 20 cm
Western Zhou Dynasty (ca. 1100-771 BC)
Found at Yangjiabu Village in Fufeng County, Shaanxi Province.
Shaanxi Fufeng County Museum

24

Inner Chariot Axle Cover

Bronze; l. 20.5 cm
Western Zhou Dynasty (ca. 1100-771 BC)
Found in 1980 at Zhuyuangou in Baoji City, Shaanxi Province.
Shaanxi Baoji Municipal Museum

25

Inner Chariot Axle Covers

Bronze; l. 17.2 cm
Western Zhou Dynasty (ca. 1100-771 BC)
Found in 1980 at Zhuyuangou in Baoji City, Shaanxi Province.
Shaanxi Baoji Municipal Museum

26

Inner Chariot Axle Cover

Bronze; l. 21.6 cm
Western Zhou Dynasty (ca. 1100-771 BC)
Discovered at Jingdang Town in Qishan County in Shaanxi Province.
Zhouyuan Museum of Qishan County

27
Pipe-Handled Chariot Bell
Bronze; h. 11.5 cm
Western Zhou Dynasty (ca. 1100-771 BC)
Excavated at Changqing Town in Fengxiang,
Shaanxi Province.
Shaanxi Fengxiang County Museum

This type of bell is extremely rare among the Western Zhou chariot and horse ornaments. It is constructed with two symmetrical holes in the shaft for attachment onto the chariot. There is a bronze ball inside the hollow-shaped bell head.

28
Four Circular Chariot Bells
Bronze; h. 17.2-18.5 cm
Western Zhou Dynasty (ca. 1100-771 BC)
Discovered at Huangdui Town in Fufeng County,
Shaanxi Province.
Shaanxi Provincial Zhouyuan Museum

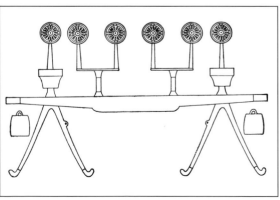

Figure 10

29

Two Axle End Covers with Circular Designs

Bronze; l. 11.8 cm, d. 6 cm
Linchpin; l. 11.2 cm
Western Zhou Dynasty (ca. 1100-771 BC)
Excavated in 1980 at Huangdui Town in Fufeng County, Shaanxi Province.
Shaanxi Provincial Zhouyuan Museum

The two axle end covers decorated with a serpentine wave pattern (*huandai*) and "impoverished" curves (*qiequ*) designs with linchpins.

30

Axle End Cover Depicting an "Animal Eating A Man"

Bronze; l. 11.5 cm, d. 5.6 cm
Linchpin; l. 10.3 cm
Western Zhou Dynasty (ca. 1100-771 BC)
Excavated in 1980at Huangdui Town in Fufeng County, Shaanxi Province.
Shaanxi Provincial Zhouyuan Museum

This axle end cover was held in place by a linchpin featuring a tiger's head at the top of the pin.

31

Two Axle End Covers

Bronze; l. 15.7 cm, d. 5.4 cm
Western Zhou Dynasty (ca. 1100-771 BC)
Excavated in 1980 at Zhuyuangou in Baoji City, Shaanxi Province.
Shaanxi Baoji Municipal Museum

These axle end covers feature "banana leaf" design and have tiger-head linchpins.

32
Two Geometric Frontlets
Bronze; h. 18.5 cm
Western Zhou Dynasty (ca. 1100-771 BC)
Excavated in 1980 at Zhuyuangou in Baoji City,
Shaanxi Province.
Shaanxi Baoji Municipal Museum

33
Arrow with Branches Frontlet
Bronze; h. 25.5 cm
Western Zhou Dynasty (ca. 1100-771 BC)
Excavated in Fengming Town in Qishan County in
Shaanxi Province.
Shaanxi Qishan County Museum

These face ornaments for horses fall into four categories: (1) "Y" shaped frontlets with rounded domes in the middle and lower parts, (2) elongated frontlets incised with animal faces or designs, (3) thin, elongated strips with incised animal faces at the top and bottom and (4) particularly long frontlets featuring a circular disk with two knife-like "ears" projecting from the top. The first and second were common in the Western Zhou Dynasty while the third and the fourth types were quite rare in that period.

34
Animal Face Frontlets
Bronze; h. 30.5 cm
Western Zhou Dynasty (ca. 1100-771 BC)
Excavated in Fufeng County, Shaanxi Province.
Shaanxi Provincial Zhouyuan Museum

35
Goat or Ram Head Frontlets
Bronze; h. 21.8 cm
Western Zhou Dynasty (ca. 1100-771 BC)
Excavated in 1980 at Zhuyuangou in Baoji City, Shaanxi Province.
Shaanxi Baoji Municipal Museum

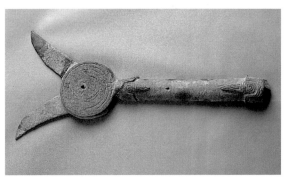

36
Y-Shaped Frontlet
Bronze; h. 36.5 cm
Western Zhou Dynasty (ca. 1100-771 BC)
Excavated in Fufeng County, Shaanxi Province.
Shaanxi Fufeng County Museum

37

Two Coiled Snake Bits

Bronze; d. 9.2 cm
Western Zhou Dynasty (ca. 1100-771 BC)
Excavated in 1980 at Zhuyuangou in Baoji City,
Shaanxi Province.
Shaanxi Baoji Municipal Museum

The circular cheek pieces of these bits depict snakes and have a decorative swirling design. The cheek pieces are hollow circles with four small hollow cylinders attached to the back through which leather thongs could be threaded. The mouthpieces are two linked bronze figure eight shaped pieces that appear very angular and suggest these may have been decorative pieces rather than bits actually used on horses.

38

"Pistol-Handle" Shaped Cheek Pieces

Bronze; l. 15 cm
Western Zhou Dynasty (ca. 1100-771 BC)
Discovered in Fufeng County, Shaanxi Province.
Shaanxi Provincial Zhouyan Museum

The two pair of hooked or pistol-handle shaped cheek pieces are decorated with animal heads that encircle the hole where the now missing mouthpiece would have been attached.

39
Rectangular Cheeked Bit

Bronze; l. 7.9 cm, w. 7.3 cm
Western Zhou Dynasty (ca. 1100-771 BC)
Found at Yuntang Village in Fufeng County, Shaanxi Province.
Shaanxi Fufeng County Museum

The rectangular cheek pieces are all that remain of this bit. The round holes in the center would have held the missing mouthpiece; and the reins and headstall of the bridle would have been attached to the rectangular slot on the side. Relatively plain rectangular cheek pieces were used from the late Shang dynasty.

40
Loose-Cheek Snaffle Bit

Bronze; l. 14 cm, w. 20 cm
Western Zhou Dynasty (ca. 1100-771 BC)
Found at Yuntang Village in Fufeng County, Shaanxi Province.
Shaanxi Fufeng County Museum

The jointed mouthpiece of this bit has rings on each end that allows the branch shaped cheek pieces to slide and adjust slightly to the pull of the reins.

41
Curb Chain Fragment

Bronze; l. 21 cm
Western Zhou Dynasty (ca. 1100-771 BC)
Found at Yuntang Village in Fufeng County, Shaanxi Province.
Shaanxi Fufeng County Museum

The four granular textured links that remain of this bridle part were originally fitted with buckles on both ends. The textured surface, length and flexibility of the chain suggest its use as a curb chain rather than a bit.

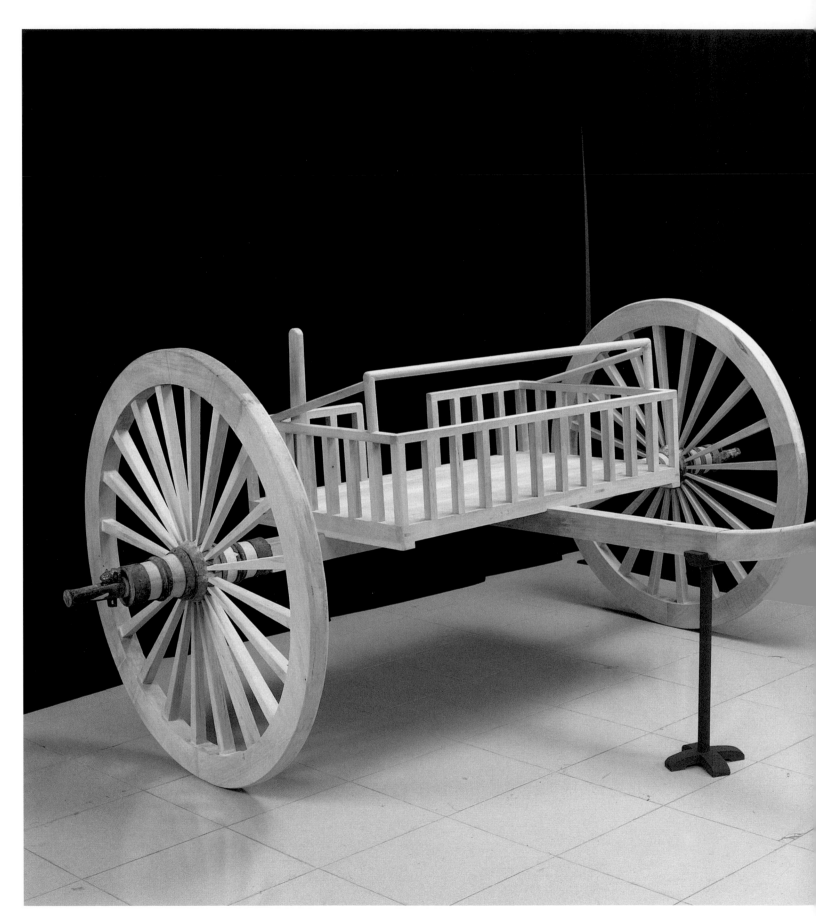

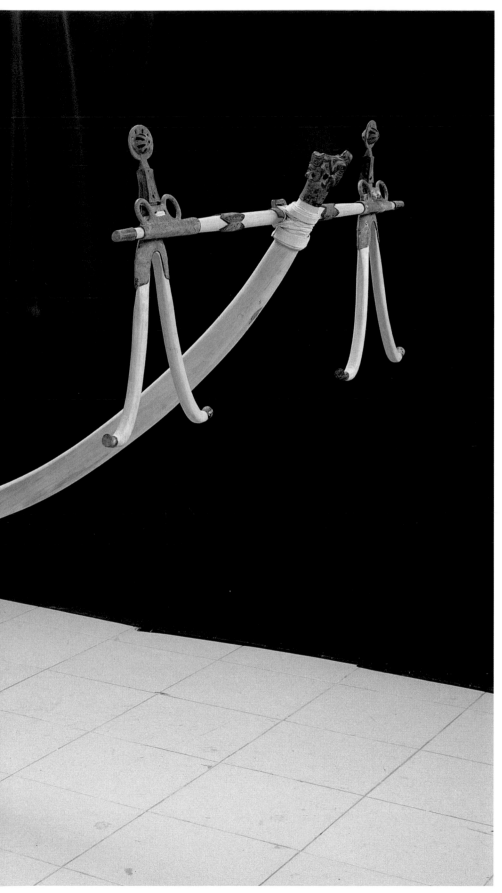

42

Reconstructed Wooden Chariot with Original Bronze Fittings
Bronze
Western Zhou Dynasty (ca. 1100-771 BC)
Excavated in 1974 at Rujiazhuang Village, Baoji City, Shaanxi Province.
Baoji Municipal City Museum

This reconstructed Western Zhou dynasty chariot is a beautiful example of a horse drawn vehicle used for special occasions by the nobility. The original bronze fittings include bells, axle end-caps, linchpins, yoke, pole, and chariot body decorations. A total of 33 bronze fittings were used in the reassembled vehicle. Precise measurements of the depressions left by the wooden components of the chariot have allowed for the accurate reconstruction of this lightweight and elegant chariot. The wheels each have 20 spokes, a diameter of 1.2 meters, and sturdy rims. Note the graceful curve of the pole, and the understated decoration of the bronze fittings. This chariot is being shown for the first time ever in this exhibition. It was reconstructed in 1999 by Chinese craftsmen, under the direction of archaeologists from throughout China.

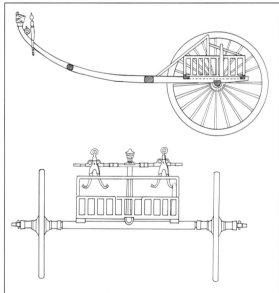

Figure 10

The reconstruction of this chariot was made possible through the support of the International Museum of the Horse, the Kentucky Horse Park, and the Kentucky Horse Park Foundation.

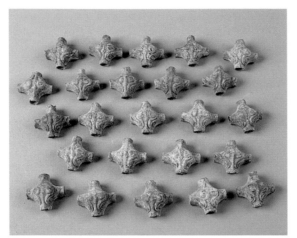

43
Harness Links

Bronze; l. 4 cm, w. 4.6 cm
Western Zhou Dynasty (ca. 1100-771 BC)
Excavated in 1980 at Zhuyuangou in Baoji City,
Shaanxi Province.
Shaanxi Baoji Municipal Museum

These twenty-four bronze harness links are hollow, open on the underside and were strategically placed where two straps intersect on the rigging of the horse's gear. They have raised goat heads with curled horns as their decoration. These connectors were found with remnants of leather thongs remaining in the cavities where they were preserved by association with the bronze.

44
Two-Handled Food Container (*Gui*)

Bronze; h. 25.9 cm, d. 19.7 cm
Western Zhou Dynasty (ca. 1100-771 BC)
Excavated in 1980 at Zhuyuangou, Baoji City,
Shaanxi Province.
Baoji Municipal City Museum

This food container or gui was traditionally used for storage of sorghum, millet, rice and other grains. During the Western Zhou dynasty, vessels of this type also served as sacrificial vessels. Inside the square base hangs a bronze bell. The walls of the vessel and the base are covered with *taotie* (ogre-mask) designs. Its handles are decorated with rabbits.

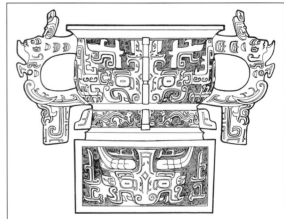

Figure 12

The craftsmen of the Shang dynasty had been masters of creating intricate and complex works of bronze. The Western and Eastern Zhou inherited their skills, but over time would gradually simplify the intricacies shown in both the shape and decoration of their predecessors bronze work.

45

Four-Handled Food Container
(*Gui*)

Bronze; h. 23.8 cm, d. 26.8 cm
Western Zhou Dynasty (ca. 1100-771 BC)
Excavated in 1981 at Zhifangtou in Baoji City,
Shaanxi Province.
Shaanxi Baoji City Municipal Museum

This food container also served as a sacrificial vessel of
a nobleman. It is quite deep with a round base and a
large mouth. The body is decorated with seven lines of
yuanru, or raised dots; with a band of vertical bars that
circle the center. Its base is embellished with *taotie*
(ogre-mask) designs. The handles, or ears, of the vessel
are mounted with oxen heads between whose horns are
visible smaller oxen heads.

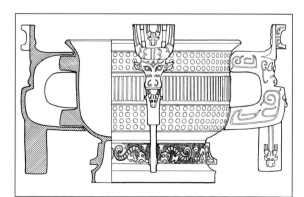

Figure 13

46
Wine Cup with Curved Handles

Bronze; h. 14 cm, d. 10.8 cm
Western Zhou (ca. 1100-771 BC)
Unearthed in 1975 at Zhuangbai Village in Fufeng
County, Shaanxi Province.
Shaanxi Fufeng County Museum

This cup was the first excavated wine utensil of its kind from the Shang or Zhou dynasties. It has two trunk-like handles. The neck is decorated with phoenix designs and thunder pattern lines enhance the handles. On the bottom of the interior are incised five Chinese characters which read: "It was made by Bodong."

47
Dragon Wine Cup

Bronze; h. 12.2 cm, d. 5 cm
Western Zhou Dynasty (ca. 1100-771 BC)
Excavated in 1961 at Zhangjiapo in Chang'an County,
Shaanxi Province.
Shaanxi History Museum

This two-handled wine cup has an open flared mouth with a raised band around the center. The handles, or ears, are in a very stylized dragon motif.

48
Wine Cup with Single Handle

Bronze; h. 13.3 cm, d. 11.8 cm
Western Zhou Dynasty (ca. 1100-771 BC)
Excavated in 1961 at Zhangjiapo in Chang'an County,
Shaanxi Province.
Shaanxi History Museum

The simple lines of this cup are quite different from the other vessels in this exhibit. Its delicately curved body is offset by the bold geometry of the handle. Other than the five holes that pierce the handle, it is devoid of decorative embellishment.

49

Crawling Dragon

Bronze; l. 60 cm
Western Zhou Dynasty (ca. 1100-771 BC)
Excavated in 1993 at Shaogong Town in Fufeng County,
Shaanxi Province.
Shaanxi Fufeng County Museum

This dragon is exquisitely designed with prominent
horns, dagger-like eyebrows, and bulging eyes. Its
mouth is open and we can see two teeth. The horns are
embellished with *yuanwo*, (whorl pattern), and *xuanwen*,
(bowstring pattern) designs. Its legs are damaged
which suggest it was once a part of a larger bronze
vessel.

50
Bird Wine Vessel

Bronze; h. 23 cm, l. 30 cm, w. 10.6 cm
Western Zhou Dynasty (ca. 1100-771 BC)
Excavated in 1974 at Rujia Village in Baoji City,
Shaanxi Province.
Shaanxi Baoji Municipal Museum

Birds were popular diversions for the nobility during the Western Zhou dynasty. This rare bronze example stands solidly, looking into the distance. Incised lines suggest feathers and wings, but the three large feet give it a flightless feel. (Fig. 14) The design may be based on a Chinese fairytale about a three-legged green bird able to stand without difficulty. It was excavated from the tomb of Duke Yu, a nobleman who lived during the reign of King Mu (1001-947 BC).

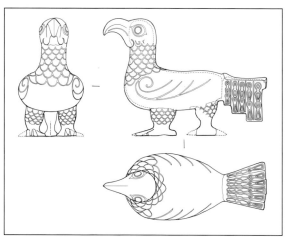

Figure 14

51
Fish-Shaped Wine Vessel

Bronze; h. 15 cm, l. 28 cm
Western Zhou Dynasty (ca. 1100-771 BC)
Excavated in 1988 at Rujia Village of Baoji City,
Shaanxi Province.
Shaanxi Baoji Municipal Museum

Many bronze vessels shaped like sheep, oxen, elephants, etc., have been excavated from burial sites in China, but this bronze wine vessel in a fish shape is unique. It appears to be a carp, an oriental symbol of male fertility. The mouth has an opening in the lower lip for pouring the wine, while on the back is a lid to accept the wine. The vessel is supported by four human shaped figures that bend their bodies as if they were carrying a heavy weight.

52

Tiger with Cub

Bronze; h. 10 cm, l. 20 cm
Western Zhou Dynasty (ca. 1100-771 BC)
Excavated in 1988 at Rujia Village in Baoji City,
Shaanxi Province.
Shaanxi Baoji Municipal Museum

This remarkable work is an extremely rare example of craftsmanship showing the mother's love for her cub. The mother tiger has its ears raised and its eyes bulge out. It carries the cub in its mouth. The overall incised design gives the work a sense of controlled execution and adds to its playfulness.

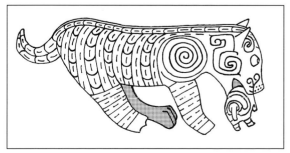

Figure 15

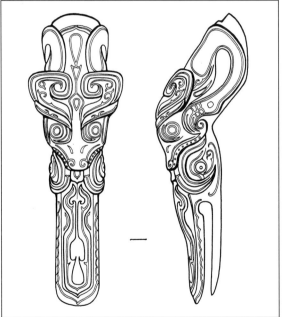

53

Flagstaff End Cap

Bronze; l. 18.5 cm
Western Zhou Dynasty (ca. 1100-771 BC)
Excavated in 1980 at Zhuyuangou in Baoji City,
Shaanxi Province.
Shaanxi Baoji Municipal Museum

These two bronze caps decorated the pole of a flag or banner used to signify the status of an important individual. (Fig. 16) The nobility used flags, sometimes embellished by yak tails, as symbols of power. The flagstaff's head is shaped like a duck, with its mouth slightly open. On its head is an animal mask, similar to the ones found buried with chariot horses. The round eyes, protruding eyebrows, and curling ears of the mask are placed on the forehead of the duck, just above the eyes. The staff end cap is decorated with phoenix designs and leaves or petals.

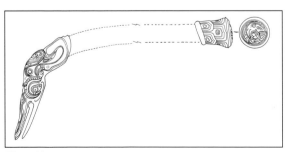

Figure 16

54

Two Spoons

Bronze; l. 3.5 cm
Western Zhou Dynasty (ca. 1100-771 BC)
Excavated in 1976 at Zhuangbai Village in Fugeng County, Shaanxi Province.
Shaanxi Provincial Zhouyuan Museum

The shafts of the handles of these spoons are twisted and decorated with stylized animal heads. Inscribed on the pointed heads of the spoons are five Chinese characters indicating that they were "made by Boxing."

55

Baigongfu Spoons

Bronze; l. 6.8 cm, d. 9.5 cm
Western Zhou Dynasty (ca. 1100-771 BC)
Excavated in 1976 at Zhuangbai Village in Fufeng County, Shaanxi Province.
Shaanxi Provincial Zhouyuan Museum

In spite of their name, these spoons are actually wine vessels (*jue*). Their decorative designs include *chanwen*, (cicada pattern), *wowen* (tile pattern), and fish scales. On the handles are twenty-eight Chinese characters indicating that these wine vessels were "made by Bofu to pray for the longevity and the happiness of his children."

56

Bronze Wine Dippers

(1) Bronze; l. 36.4 cm, d. 5 cm
(2) Bronze; l. 30.2 cm, d. 4.3 cm
(3) Bronze; l. 22.7 cm, d. 2.3 cm
(4) Bronze; l. 20.6 cm, d. 2.5 cm
Western Zhou Dynasty (ca. 1100-771 BC)
Excavated in 1976 at Zhuangbai Village in Fufeng County, Shaanxi Province.
Shaanxi Provincial Zhouyuan Museum

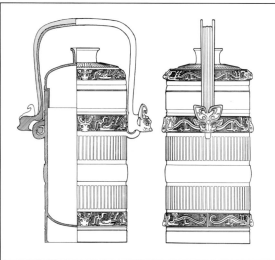

Figure 17

57

Loop-Handled Wine Vessels

(1) Bronze; h. 33.3 cm, d. 12.4 cm
(2) Bronze; h. 27 cm, d. 10.1 cm
Western Zhou Dynasty (ca. 1100-771 BC)
Excavated in 1980 at Zhuyuangou in Baoji City,
Shaanxi Province.
Shaanxi Baoji Municipal Museum

These wine vessels were made as sacrificial articles.
They are identical in design and decoration, and differ
only in size. On the bottom ends of the loop handles are
animal heads. The cylindrical bodies of the vessels are
banded with unique designs of phoenix with fallen
crests, curled tails, hooked beaks, and sharp claws.
These are very rare examples of bronze ware with
splendid but uncomplicated designs.

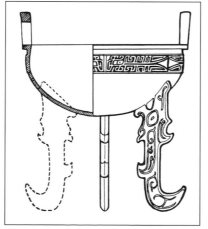

Figure 18

58

Three-Footed Tripod, (*Ding*)

Bronze; h. 16.3 cm, d. 13.5 cm
Western Zhou Dynasty (ca. 1100-771 BC)
Excavated in 1980 at Zhuyuangou in Baoji City,
Shaanxi Province.
Shaanxi Baoji Municipal Museum

This tripod was used for cooking or at sacrificial ceremonies. Unique among bronzeware from this period, it
has two standing loops or ears attached to the rim. The
three feet are in the shape of dragons with curled tails.
The bowl is decorated with a circle of *taotie* (ogre-mask)
designs. Inside the bowl is an inscribed Chinese character which literally means "dagger-axe." The splayed
shape of the feet of the tripod allowed the piece to be
placed over a small fire.

59
Wine Container (*Zun*)
Bronze; h. 22.1 cm, d. 19.5 cm
Western Zhou Dynasty (ca. 1100-771 BC)
Excavated in 1980 at Zhuyuangou in Baoji City,
Shaanxi Province.
Shaanxi Baoji Municipal Museum

The middle section of the vessel is decorated with eight groups of dragon and phoenix designs. Other designs include *xuanwen* (bowstring pattern) and *leiwen* (thunder pattern). At the bottom of the vessel is an inscription of six Chinese characters in two lines saying "Made by Yuji."

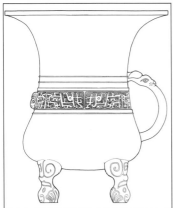

Figure 18

60
Food Container (*Fu*)
Bronze; h. 19.6 cm, l. 28.4 cm, w. 23 cm
Western Zhou Dynasty (ca. 1100-771 BC)
Excavated in 1978 at Yutang Village in Fufeng County,
Shaanxi Province.
Shaanxi Provincial Zhouyuan Museum

The top and bottom sections are identical. Each section has two ring-shaped ears or handles. Between its lid and body are four catches shaped like oxen heads. The decorative designs are overlapping rings, fish scales, *qiequ* (impoverished curves) and *huaidai* (wave pattern) designs. A highly decorative wave design runs around the both sections. The feet of the vessels are covered with shield-like designs. There is a sixty-one Chinese character inscription saying that the pot was made by Bogonfu for the storage of grains.

61
Food Vessels (*Fu*)
Bronze; h. 21.5 cm, l. 25 cm, w. 16.8 cm
Western Zhou Dynasty (ca. 1100-771 BC)
Excavated at Yuntang Village in Fufeng County,
Shaanxi Province in 1976.
Shaanxi Provincial Zhouyuan Museum

These two vessels are identical. Inscriptions note that they were made by Boduofu. The decorative designs include *qiequ* (impoverished curves) and *wawen* (tile pattern). The tops, when inverted, became serving platters, while the bottoms were used for cooking. The inverted feet provided a base for the serving portion of these vessels. They are richly ornamented with decorative designs and are in remarkably good condition given their age. Such vessels became popular in the late Western Zhou dynasty not only for the storage of rice, millet and sorghum but also for use at sacrificial ceremonies.

62
Animal-Faced Harness Decoration
Set of nineteen pieces
Bronze; h. 3-5 cm, w. 2.5-4.5 cm
Eastern Zhou Dynasty, Spring & Autumn Period
(770-476 BC)
Excavated at Bianjiazhuang Village in Longxian County,
Shaanxi Province in 1986.
Shaanxi Longxian County Museum

These animal-faced bronzes are similar in design, but of different sizes. The animal faces are like beetle shells. They have round eyes and raised horns. At the back of each piece is a flat bar, through which a leather strip could be threaded for use in horse harness decorations.

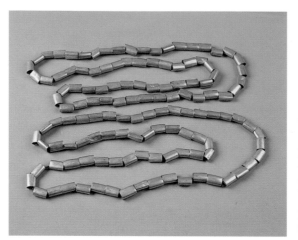

63
Chained Ornament
Gold; wt. 960 grams
Eastern Zhou Dynasty, Spring & Autumn Period
(770-476 BC)
Excavated at Yimen in 1992 in Baoji City,
Shaanxi Province.
Shaanxi Baoji Archaeological Team

There are one hundred and thirty gold tubes chained together in these two rings. They are hollow allowing leather straps to be passed through them. The original use of such tubing, which usually made of bronze, was probably to protect the reins from being severed by a sword. Gold tubing such as these are very rare, and probably served a decorative purpose due to the softness of the metal.

64
Belt Buckles
(1A) Gold; h. 1.5 cm, l. 0.6 cm
(1B) Gold; h. 2.3 cm, l. 1.7 cm
(2) Gold; h. 1.6 cm, d. 0.5 cm
Eastern Zhou Dynasty, Spring & Autumn Period
(770-476 BC)
Excavated at Yimencun Village in Baoji City,
Shaanxi Province in 1992.
Shaanxi Baoji Archaeological Team

The gold buckles fall into two types: the mandarin duck and the curling snake. The former has eyes, and the cap is inlaid with turquoise. The latter is hollow with the snake's head serving as the prong for the buckle. The lost wax casting process was used in the making of both kinds of buckles. These exceedingly fine examples of ancient goldsmith's workmanship are rarely found in Chinese burial sites.

65

Gold-Handled Sword

Gold and Iron; Hilt l. 12.7 cm, Blade l. 24.5 cm, w. 4 cm
Eastern Zhou Dynasty, Spring & Autumn Period
(770-476 BC)
Excavated at Yimencun Village in 1992 in Baoji City,
Shaanxi Province.
Shaanxi Baoji Archaeological Team

This sword has an iron blade and a gold handle or hilt
inlaid with turquoise. When the sword was unearthed
it had remnants of fabric around it and seven small
gold decorative items in a line. These would have been
attached to the fabric that served as the dagger's sheath.
The hollow hilt has identical interlaced dragon designs
on both sides. Hilts of this shape were commonly found
in Central Asia. As gold is such a soft metal, this sword
would have been impractical for use in battle, and created specifically to be buried with its owner.

66
Duck-Headed Bronze Harness Buckles

Bronze; h. 0.9 cm, d. 1.9-2.2 cm
Eastern Zhou Dynasty, Spring & Autumn Period
(770-476 BC)
Excavated in 1992 at Yimen Town in Baoji City,
Shaanxi Province.
Shaanxi Baoji Municipal Archaeological Team

All of these buckles were designed in the shape of rings with duck head clasps. The duck head has a short neck and flat bill. They were both practical and decorative, and were probably used as strap buckles for the horse's harness.

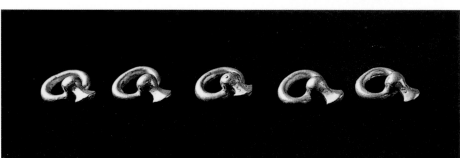

67
Duck-Headed Gold Harness Buckles

Gold; h. 0.9 cm, d. 1.3 cm
Eastern Zhou Dynasty, Spring & Autumn Period
(770-476 BC)
Excavated in 1992 at Yimen Town in Baoji City,
Shaanxi Province.
Shaanxi Baoji Municipal Archaeological Team

68
Duck-Headed Jade Buckle

Jade; h. 1.6 cm, l. 6 cm
Eastern Zhou Dynasty, Spring & Autumn Period
(770-476 BC)
Excavated in 1992 at Yimen Town in Baoji City,
Shaanxi Province.
Shaanxi Baoji Municipal Archaeological Team

69
Jade Horse Head

Jade; l. 5.5 cm, w. 5.5 cm, d. 0.3 cm
Eastern Zhou Dynasty, Spring & Autumn Period
(770-476 BC)
Excavated in 1986 from Number 1 Qingong Tomb in
Fengxiang County, Shaanxi Province.
Shaanxi History Museum

The horse's head is made of polished black jade with carved eyes and bridle. Under the head are four regularly shaped holes, one being damaged and one being incomplete. Judging from the four holes, there should have been a wooden handle. This object was most probably used as a sacrificial article.

70
Gold Dog
Gold; h. 1.7 cm, l. 3.5 cm
Eastern Zhou Dynasty, Spring & Autumn Period
(770-476 BC)
Excavated in 1986 from Number 1 Qingong Tomb in
Fengxiang County, Shaanxi Province.
Shaanxi History Museum

This crouching dog was made by die-casting. Its joints,
feet and tail are accented with designs of juanyun, or
curling clouds. It is representative of the gold decorations found in the early Qin kingdom which was noted
for its simple designs. As the Qin people came from the
west, much of their art reflects the traditions of the
Xiongnu and other nomadic steppe tribes.

71
Gold Tiger Harness Ornament
Gold; l. 4.5 cm, w. 0.5 cm
Eastern Zhou Dynasty, Spring & Autumn Period
(770-476 BC)
Excavated in 1991 at Weijiaya in Baoji City,
Shaanxi Province.
Shaanxi Baoji County Museum

This tiger is made of gold and weighs only 30 grams,
but it looks powerful and mighty with strong legs. The
crouching tiger has its mouth agape, showing its teeth,
and its ears are pointed up. At the back is a bar to
which a leather strap could be attached for use as a harness ornament.

Figure 20

72

Harness Ornaments

Gold with Bronze Ring; l. 2.8 cm, ring d. 4.7 cm
Eastern Zhou Dynasty, Spring & Autumn Period
(770-476 BC)
Excavated in l986 from the Qingong Tomb, pit no. 1,
Fengxiang County, Shaanxi Province.
Shaanxi Provincial Archaeological Research Institute

The ornaments are made of pure gold, and are free of
any decorative designs. (Fig. 20) One of them has a
bronze ring without any decorative treatment. They
would have been used for harness decorations with
leather thongs threaded through them.

73

Mythical Beast Chariot Pole Ornament

Gold; h. 2.4 cm, l. 3.7 cm
Eastern Zhou Dynasty, Spring & Autumn Period
(770-476 BC)
Excavated from the temple ruins at Majiazhuang Village
in Fengxiang County, Shaanxi Province.
Shaanxi History Museum

This mythical golden beast combines a tiger's head
with the horns of a sheep and two wings. Circular
engravings are used on the head and limbs. (The body
was made by relief sculpture.) The piece was used as
an ornament for a chariot pole. On the back is a device
used to connect it to the chariot. This beast is representative of the decorative arts of the period.

74

Harness Buckle

Gold; l. 4 cm, w. 3.3 cm
Qin Dynasty (221-207 BC)
Excavated at Lanfucun Village in Fengxiang County,
Shaanxi Province.
Shaanxi Fengxiang County Museum

Recessed in a framework of twisting snakes, this gold
buckle has an animal face with two protruding eyes,
curled horns and a long tongue sticking out of its
mouth. At the back of this buckle are two buttons, onto
which leather straps would be affixed.

75
Harness Buttons or Rosettes
Set of nine pieces, Bronze
(1) Three Gilded Bronze Decorations; d. 4.9 cm
(2) Gilded Bronze Decoration; d. 5.4 cm
(3) Five Juanyun Design Decorations, d. 2.5-4.1 cm
Qin Dynasty (221-207 BC)
Excavated at Fanjiazhai in Fengxiang County,
Shaanxi Province.
Shaanxi Fengxiang County Museum

The reverse sides of these gilded bronze ware ornaments have semicircular buttons, onto which one could
tie leather straps. The recognizable motif of a realistic
bear head adorns one of these decorative buttons (2).
The others are covered with swirling *juanyun*, or curling cloud designs, and have bars on the backs so that
leather thongs can be attached to them.

76
Bridle Rosettes
Five Gold Animal Face Ornaments
Gold; h. 2.2 cm, w. 3.5 cm
Eastern Zhou Dynasty, Spring & Autumn Period
(770-476 BC)
Excavated in 1992 at Yimen Town in Baoji City,
Shaanxi Province.
Shaanxi Baoji Municipal Archaeological Research Institute

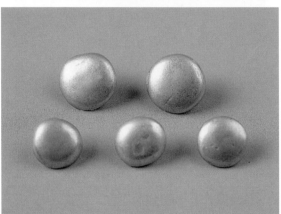

77
Gold Harness Ornaments
Gold; d. 2-3.2 cm
Eastern Zhou Dynasty, Spring & Autumn Period
(770-476 BC)
Excavated in 1992 at Yimen Town in Baoji City,
Shaanxi Province.
Shaanxi Baoji Municipal Archaeological Research Institute

78
Mythical Beast Ornaments
Gold; l. 2.2 cm, w. 1.7 cm
Eastern Zhou Dynasty, Spring & Autumn Period
(770-476 BC)
Excavated in 1982 at Majiazhuang Village in
Fengxiang County, Shaanxi Province.
Shaanxi Baoji Municipal Archaeological Research Institute

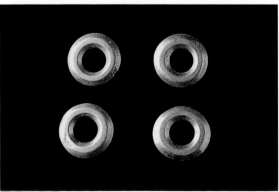

79
Gold Rings
Gold; outer diam. 3.1 cm, inner diam. 1.5 cm
Eastern Zhou Dynasty, Spring & Autumn Period
(770-476 BC)
Excavated in 1992 at Yimen at Baoji City, Shaanxi Province.
Shaanxi Baoji Municipal Archaeological Team

These gold rings share the same size and shape. Their cross section is hexagonal, which gives them a finely crafted appearance. Bronze rings were commonly used in Chinese horse decorations, but gold rings are very unusual. These were held to the harness by leather straps.

80

Hook-Shaped Chariot Ornaments

Bronze; l. 16.9 cm, h. 6.9 cm
Eastern Zhou Dynasty, Spring & Autumn Period
(770-476 BC)
Excavated in 1986 at Bianjiazhuang in Longxian County,
Shaanxi Province.
Shaanxi Longxian County Museum

These ornaments have small animal heads with protruding eyes and horns that turn downwards. The two
horn shaped ends turn upwards. Between the two
horns are two small round holes by which these ornaments were attached to a wooden frame with a rivet,
perhaps as a part of a chariot's decoration.

81

Bronze Chariot Ornaments

Bronze; l. 3.2 cm
Eastern Zhou Dynasty, Spring & Autumn Period
(770-476 BC)
Excavated at Bianjiazhuang Village in Longxian County,
Shaanxi Province in 1986.
Shaanxi Longxian County Museum

The triangular ornaments look like moths with pierced
heads and wings. They were originally affixed to a
nobleman's chariot.

82

Bronze Chariot Ornaments

Bronze; h. 2.5 cm, l. 3.4 cm
Eastern Zhou Dynasty, Spring & Autumn Period
(770-476 BC)
Excavated at Bianjiazhuang Village in Longxian County,
Shaanxi Province in 1986.
Shaanxi Longxian County Museum

The rabbits that decorate these ornaments are sitting
crouched on their legs, with their eyes wide open and
their ears turned backwards. Their feet are pierced to
allow fastening to the wooden frame of a chariot.

83

Axle Heads or End Caps
Bronze; h. 11.5 cm, d. 5 cm
Eastern Zhou Dynasty, Spring & Autumn Period
(770-476 BC)
Excavated in 1986 at Bianjiazhuang in Longxian County,
Shaanxi Province.
Shaanxi Longxian County Museum

These bronze axle heads were used to secure the wheel
to the chariot axle. The axle head is cylindrical, with the
thicker end enveloping the axle. They are decorated
with impoverished curve motifs (*tiequ*) and double ring
designs (*chonghuan*).

84

Yunwen Axle Head or End Cap
Bronze; h. 6.8 cm, d. 8.4 cm
Eastern Zhou Dynasty, Spring & Autumn Period
(770-476 BC)
Excavated in 1986 at Bianjiazhuang in Longxian County,
Shaanxi Province.
Shaanxi Longxian County Museum

This bronze axle head, used to secure the wheel to the
chariot axle, is embellished with cloud patterns and
edges (*tuxuan*). It was secured on the protruding end
of the axle with a linchpin.

85
Hepan Drinking Vessels & Saucers
(1) Bronze; h. 14 cm, w. 16 cm
(2) Bronze; h. 14.4 cm, w. 14.3 cm
(3) Bronze; h. 8.7 cm, d. 23.5 cm
(4) Bronze; h. 8.5 cm, d. 19 cm
Eastern Zhou Dynasty, Spring & Autumn Period
(770-476 BC)
Excavated in 1981 at Bianjiacun Village County,
Shaanxi Province.
Shaanxi Longxian County Museum

The prototype for these vessels, the *heh*, was a three-legged bronze container popular during the Shang and Zhou dynasties used to heat wine. By the Spring and Autumn period, however, these examples had become flatter and thinner, and had gradually lost their function of heating wine. Each container has a spout on the front, an animal head handle on the back, and a bird-shaped decorative piece on the top. The two saucers were very fashionable during the Spring and Autumn period, and are identical, having rounded bases and handles or ears for lifting. These vessels are small in size and intended to be used as burial objects.

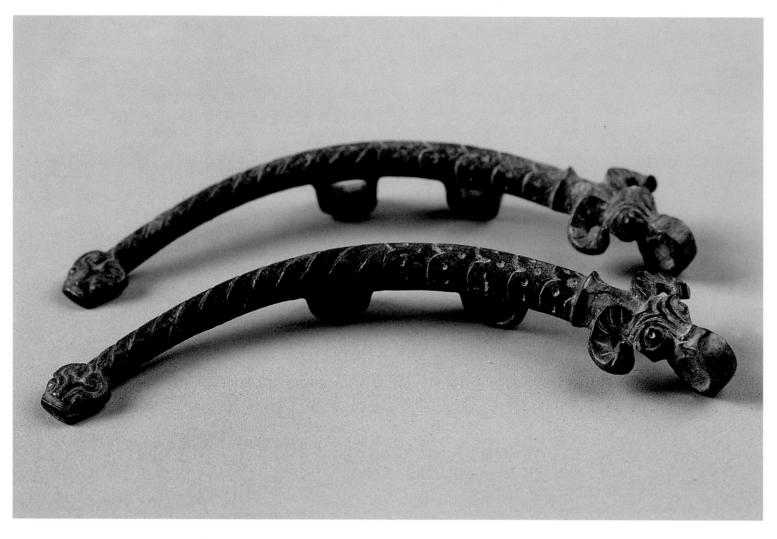

86

Ram's Head Bit Cheek Pieces

Bronze; l. 13 cm
Eastern Zhou Dynasty, Spring & Autumn Period
(770-476 BC)
Excavated in Baoji County, Shaanxi Province.
Shaanxi Baoji County Museum

These bridle cheek pieces, which were popular in the
Spring & Autumn period, are long and arched, topped
with a ram's head motif featuring round eyes and horns
which curve outwards. The mouthpiece of the bit, now
missing, would have attached to the rings on the end of
the cheek pieces and the headstall and rein straps to the
other two loops.

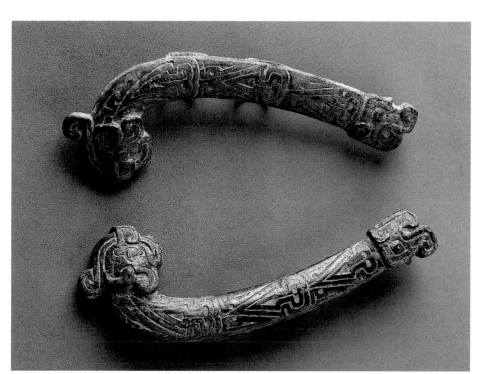

87
Dragon Bit Cheek Pieces
Bronze; l. 11 cm
Eastern Zhou Dynasty, Spring & Autumn Period
(770-476 BC)
Excavated at Bianjiazhung in Longxian County,
Shaanxi Province in 1968.
Shaanxi Longxian County Museum

These cheek pieces, shaped like hooks with dragons
heads turned to the side, are heavily decorated with
intertwined incised lines. There are two loops on the
back for attachment of the reins and headstall.

88
Loose-Ring Dragon Bit Cheek Pieces
Bronze; l. 13.5 cm
Eastern Zhou Dynasty, Spring & Autumn Period
(770-476 BC)
Excavated at Bianjiazhung in Longxian County,
Shaanxi Province in 1968.
Shaanxi Longxian County Museum

Heavily decorated with interlocking motifs that run the
length of the dragon's body, these bit cheek pieces
would have allowed the mouthpiece, now missing, to
move and adjust to the movement of the horse.

89
Jieyue Links
Set of twelve pieces
Bronze; 3.4-4.6 cm
Eastern Zhou Dynasty, Spring & Autumn Period
(770-476 BC)
Excavated at Bianjiazhuang in Longxian County,
Shaanxi Province in l986.
Shaanxi Longxian County Museum

These bronze links were used to control the direction of leather bands or straps on the harness. They are hollow, and are either "+" shaped or "x" shaped. The opposite sides are decorated with either cicada (chanwen) designs or animal faces.

90
Spin Shafts or Turn Buckles
Bronze; h. 5.0-5.6 cm
Eastern Zhou Dynasty, Spring & Autumn Period
(770-476 BC)
Excavated at Yimen Village in Baoji City,
Shaanxi Province in 1992.
Shaanxi Baoji Municipal Archaeological Team

These turn buckles, or spin shafts are spherical and hollow. The spheres are decorated with impoverished curve (*tiequ*) designs. They have a rotating loop on each end and were used to prevent the harness straps from twisting or becoming tangled.

91
Horse Bells
Bronze; h. 8.5 cm
Eastern Zhou Dynasty, Spring & Autumn Period
(770-476 BC)
Excavated at Bianjiazhuang in Longxian County,
Shaanxi Province in 1986.
Shaanxi Longxian County Museum

Though these bronze bells are identical in design, each is a slightly different size. Inside the crescent-shaped bells is a spherical tongue or clapper. They are embellished with cloud and thunder (*yunlei*) designs and were attached to the horse's harness.

92

Snaffle Bits

Bronze; l. 19-22 cm
Eastern Zhou Dynasty, Spring & Autumn Period
(770-476 BC)
Excavated at Yimen Village in Baoji City,
Shaanxi Province in 1992.
Shaanxi Baoji Municipal Archaeological Team

93

Horse Training Device

Bronze; l. 39.5 cm
Eastern Zhou Dynasty, Spring & Autumn Period
(770-476 BC)
Excavated in 1992 at Zhihui Village in Fengxiang County,
Shaanxi Province.
Shaanxi Fengxiang County Museum

The chained bit consists of seven interconnected segments, and has a semicircular snaffle bit with attached rods. Rings attached to the end of the bit could hold the reins allowing the rider to control the horse.

94

Axle End Cover Linchpin with Man-Tiger Design

Bronze; h. 16.3 cm
Eastern Zhou Dynasty, Spring & Autumn Period
(770-476 BC)
Excavated at Tianwang Town in Baoji County,
Shaanxi Province.
Shaanxi Baoji County Museum

The linchpin is inserted into a hole in the axle end cap to keep the wheel in place. The linchpin was secured by inserting another pin through the hole at the bottom.

95
Square-Based Incense Burner
Bronze; h. 36 cm
Eastern Zhou Dynasty, Warring States Period
(475-221 BC)
Excavated at the Yuncheng Ruins in Fengxiang County,
Shaanxi Province in 1995.
Shaanxi Fengxiang County Museum

The incense burner consists of three sections: the base, the pillar and the burner. The ball-shaped burner has an interior chamber and an exterior chamber. It is decorated with four animal heads holding rings in their mouths. Atop the burner is a standing phoenix with its wings spread and a ring in its mouth. The base is hollow.

96

A Pair of Cavalrymen

Earthenware with Painted Decorations
(1) h. 23.5 cm, l. 18 cm
(2) h. 23.5 cm, l. 17.5 cm
Eastern Zhou Dynasty, Warring States Period
(475-221 BC)
Excavated in 1995 from tomb no. 2, Xianying City,
Shaanxi Province.
Xi'an Institute Of Cultural Relics and Archaeology

These two hand-molded earthenware horses and riders are thought to be the oldest known examples of pottery cavalrymen ever found in China. The horses have painted bridles, and the figures are shown holding reins (now missing) in one hand. They also have holes in their free hands, which may have held spears or whips.

The figures are dressed in military uniforms with tunics, short trousers, rounded skullcaps and boots. The edges of their hats and tunics are decorated with red paint. These pieces would have been created shortly after the Chinese had been forced to develop their own cavalry to combat the raids of the mounted Xiongnu horsemen.

Approximately 1.25 kilometers east of the tomb of China's first emperor, Qin Shi Huang, lies one of the world's most remarkable archaeological sites - the Emperor's terracotta army. Since their discovery in 1974, more than 7,000 soldiers, horses and chariots have been unearthed. It is estimated that it required 38 years and more than 700,000 convicts to complete the army's tomb.

All of the soldiers and horses were made using local clay. The modeling, firing, and painting of the figures placed in the mausoleum required a number of steps. The clay was sifted and washed to ensure an even texture and color and was combined with ground quartz. After repeated kneading, the wet clay would achieve the right degree of firmness. The feet and the board on which they stood were molded with the legs. The torso was either sculpted from strips of clay or cast prior to the attachment of the arms. The final step was the creation of the head and hands. Each one was rough cast and then subjected to additions of ears, noses and hair which were applied with layers of clay which in turn were sculpted to create an individualized appearance for each of the figures. No two figures in the tomb have the same features or expression.

The firing of the pieces would have required exceptionally large kilns. There are estimates that to achieve the uniform results in the firing process, the temperature inside the kilns would have had to reach at least 900 degrees centigrade and possibly up to 1,000 degrees centigrade (1652-1832 degrees Fahrenheit). After firing, the figures were painted to resemble their counterparts in the actual Qin army. Colors were applied over a glue to help them to adhere to the figures. The colors used, traces of each having been found within the tomb, were: vermilion, claret, pink, greens, purple, blues, azure, yellow, orange, white and ochre, all from mineral sources.

The horses were produced in a similar fashion, having been first rough cast, with later applications of clay carved to show the details. The horse's heads were cast in two parts with ears and other elements such as harness straps, saddles, or bridles added later. The horse's muzzles were shaped by hand and applied to the molded parts of the head. The legs were tempered to ensure that they would be strong. The neck and trunk were formed from molds and attached. The horses' tails and ears were also modeled by hand. Lute (a smooth paste-like clay) was used to assemble the various parts.

High Ranking Officer

Terracotta, h. 197 cm, wt. 250 kg
Qin Dynasty (221-207 BC)
Excavated in 1977 from pit no. 2, the Necropolis of Qin
Shi Huang, Lintong County, Shaanxi Province.
Museum of the Qin Shi Huang Terracotta Army

This is one of six "generals" found with the terracotta army near the tomb of Emperor Qin Shi Huang, the first Emperor of a unified China. The officer's gesture and size give him a majestic presence. His double-layered costume, with an armored vest and headdress, are indicative of his high position and authority. These officers rode on chariots, where they could observe the battle with greater clarity, and controlled the movement of their troops with drums and bells. When the drum sounded the troops were sent into battle; when the bells rang, the troops withdrew. His carefully groomed mustache and sideburns convey a sense of authority, solemnity and dignity.

98

Kneeling Archer

Terracotta; h. 125 cm, wt. 117 kg
Qin Dynasty (221-207 BC)
Excavated in 1977 from pit no. 2, the Necropolis of Qin
Shi Huang, Lintong County, Shaanxi Province.
Museum of the Qin Shi Huang Terracotta Army

The kneeling archer is one of the most beautiful and
dramatic figures from pit no. 2. With an athletic bearing
poised for warfare, this figure shows rare traces of the
original paint on the straps connecting his armor. This
figure is shown preparing to load an arrow into his
now missing crossbow. As with all of the terracotta
figures, the archer is highly detailed, even showing the
pebbled surface texture on the soles of his shoes.

99
Charioteer

Terracotta; h. 195 cm, wt. 175 kg
Qin Dynasty (221-207 BC)
Excavated in 1977 from pit no. 2, the Necropolis of Qin
Shi Huang, Lintong County, Shaanxi Province.
Museum of the Qin Shi Huang Terracotta Army

The chariot driver or imperial charioteer (*yushou*) was provided with a special uniform with extra armor to protect his arms, hands, neck and upper body. This was necessary because he needed to use both hands to hold the reins, and thus could not defend himself.

Two chariot guards stood to the left and right of the driver and were armed with spears or pikes. These figures are shown standing with their feet placed to balance their weight while the chariot is in motion.

100
Chariot Guard (Right)
Terracotta; h. 190 cm, wt. 170 kg
Qin Dynasty (221-207 BC)
Excavated in 1977 from pit no. 2, the Necropolis of Qin Shi Huang, Lintong County, Shaanxi Province.
Museum of the Qin Shi Huang Terracotta Army

101
Chariot Guard (Left)
Terracotta; h. 193 cm, wt. 170 kg
Qin Dynasty (221-207 BC)
Excavated in 1977 from pit no. 2, the Necropolis of Qin Shi Huang, Lintong County, Shaanxi Province.
Museum of the Qin Shi Huang Terracotta Army

102
Cavalry Horse
Terracotta; h. 174 cm, l. 213 cm, wt. 340 kg
Qin Dynasty (221-207 BC)
Excavated in 1977 from pit no. 2, the Necropolis of Qin
Shi Huang, Lintong County, Shaanxi Province.
Museum of the Qin Shi Huang Terracotta Army

The horse is shown with a saddle decorated with studs, tassels, crupper and a belly band. The detailed carving of the horse is extremely fine. These sturdy horses stood approximately 13.2 hands high.

103
Cavalryman
Terracotta; h. 186 cm, wt. 184 kg
Qin Dynasty (221-207 BC)
Excavated in 1977 from pit no. 2, the Necropolis of Qin
Shi Huang, Lintong County, Shaanxi Province.
Museum of the Qin Shi Huang Terracotta Army

The cavalry was an important element of Qin Shi Huang's army, providing it with speed and agility. The cavalrymen wore short robes, an armored vest, and tight-fitting trousers. During the Qin dynasty, cavalry was still somewhat of a new phenomenon in China, where it had first gained popularity during the Warring States period. This piece represents one of the 116 cavalrymen and their horses discovered in pit no. 2.

104
Chariot Horses
All Four Horses, Terracotta; h. 171 cm, l. 213 cm, wt. 265 kg
Qin Dynasty (221-207 BC)
Excavated in 1977 from pit no. 1, the Necropolis of Qin Shi Huang, Lintong County, Shaanxi Province.
Museum of the Qin Shi Huang Terracotta Army

The four terracotta chariot horses are among the five hundred and forty horses made for the one hundred and thirty chariots placed in the terracotta army. Most of these horses were damaged when the roof of the tomb collapsed, crushing many of the figures and horses in the tomb. You will notice that there has been some reconstruction done to make these horses presentable for exhibition.

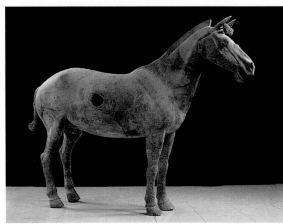

105
Kneeling Stable Boy

Terracotta; h. 68 cm
Qin Dynasty (221-207 BC)
Excavated in 1977 from the stable pit, the Necropolis of
Qin Shi Huang, Lintong County, Shaanxi Province.
Museum of the Qin Shi Huang Terracotta Army

This kneeling stable boy is shown wearing a long robe and a scarf around his neck tucked into his robe. His face has a placid expression and the hands are folded as if he awaits his next duties. The figure has his hair in a cone shaped bun at the back of his head, his face leans forward and his eyes are expressionless. He sits on his heels, a practice begun in the Shang dynasty. The practice of coiling the legs underneath the body is generally not observed in sculpture until the Tang dynasty. A stable boy's duties were to assist in raising, training and caring for the horses and birds of the Emperor.

106
Roof Tile with Chinese Character Meaning "Wagon"
Earthenware
Western Han Dynasty (206 BC–AD 8)
Excavated at Maoling, Shaanxi Province.
Shaanxi Maoling County Museum

The "wagon" character on the end of the roof tile would have indicated that the building upon which it rested housed the chariot and horse administration during the Han dynasty.

107
Roof Tile with Horse Design
Earthenware; d. 15 cm
Western Han Dynasty (206 BC–AD 8)
Excavated at Zhengji in Xi'an, Shaanxi Province.
Shaanxi Xi'an Municipal Relics Protection and Archaeological Research Center

This tile, which is decorated with a prancing horse, once graced the end of the eaves of the roof of the Emperor's stables.

108
Toilet Case
Glazed Ceramic; h. 18.7 cm, d. 18.0 cm
Western Han Dynasty (206 BC–AD 8)
Excavated in Fengxiang County, Shaanxi Province in 1975.
Shaanxi Fengxiang County Museum

This toilet case is semispherical with three legs and a lid. It was fired with contrasting colored glazes with incised decorative bands surrounding the case and swirling cloud and water (*yunshui*) pattern designs. These cases were popular, as storage vessels for women's cosmetics, mirrors, combs and other grooming articles, during the Han dynasty.

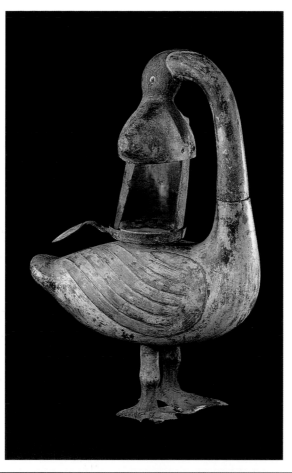

109
Goose-Fish Lamp
Bronze; h. 53 cm, l. 33 cm, w. 18 cm
Western Han Dynasty (206 BC-AD 8)
Excavated in 1985 at Dianta Village in Shenmu County,
Shaanxi Province.
Shaanxi History Museum

This oil lamp depicts a wild goose with a fish in its
mouth. In the middle of the fish's body is a hollow
cylindrical chamber into which a lamp is inserted.
When the lamp is lit, the smoke travels through the
neck and through the water filled belly where it is fil-
tered, forming an early form of pollution control. The
lamp divides into four sections, easing the cleaning
process. This is one of only two such lamps ever found
in China and is considered a national treasure.

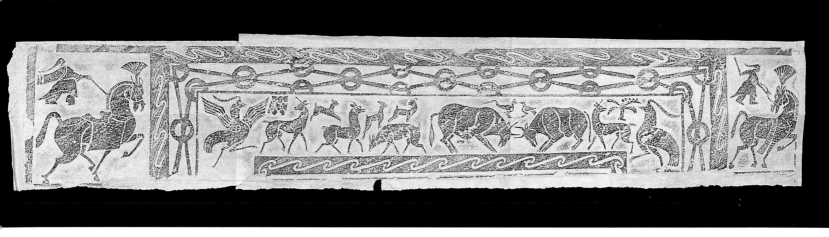

110
Tomb Door Lintel
Stone
Eastern Han Dynasty (25-220)
Excavated from the tomb of Wang Deyuan in northern
Shaanxi Province.
Shaanxi Suide County Museum

This lintel served as a horizontal stone support over the
entrance of a tomb discovered in Shaanxi Province.
Flanking the central frieze, which features a procession
of wild animals, are two paintings of horses in training.

The artist here has used incised or recessed spaces for
the background and raised areas to define the deer,
fighting bulls and other animals and birds which decorate the lintel.

111
Reconstructed Han Chariot
with Original Bronze Fittings

Reconstructed Han Chariot with Original Bronze Parts.
Bronze Inlaid with Gold
Western Han Dynasty (206 BC-AD 8)
Excavated in 1992 from the Huoqubing Tomb in Maoling,
Shaanxi Province.
Shaanxi Archaeological Research Team

This chariot has been reconstructed specifically for this exhibition utilizing all of its original bronze parts. The work was completed over the past year by a team of Chinese archaeologists and German specialists. The original excavation in 1992 provided information as to the size, function, and location of wooden parts of the chariot. These had virtually disintegrated over the past 2000 years, making their replacement necessary. The bronze pieces of the chariot feature extremely fine gold inlay and animal faces in high relief. This exhibition marks the first time that this chariot has been seen in its entirety in more than 2000 years.

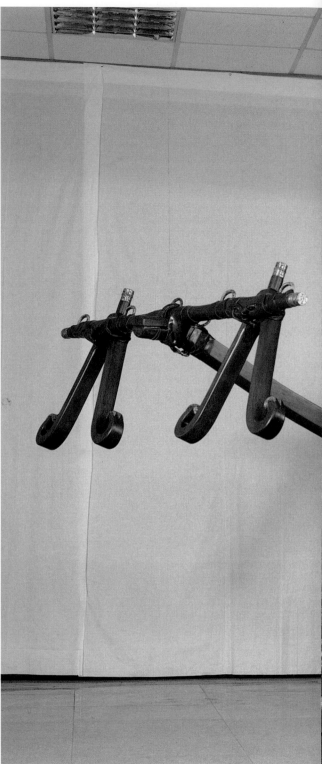

The reconstruction of this chariot was made possible through the support of the International Museum of the Horse, the Kentucky Horse Park, and the Kentucky Horse Park Foundation.

112

Tomb Door with Painted Hunting Scene

Stone; Lintel, l. 176 cm, w. 42 cm;
Frame, l. 116 cm, w. 34 cm; Doors, h. 112 cm, w 51 cm
Eastern Han Dynasty (25-220)
Excavated at Dangjiagou Village, Mizi County,
Shaanxi Province.
Shaanxi Mizhi County Relics Administration

The lintel and frame surrounding the tomb doors are covered with designs of rare birds and animals and are guarded by gods. A two storied structure is depicted on the lintel directly above the doors and contains two seated figures wearing winged capes, the dress of the immortals. To the left and right of this structure are hunting scenes with riders on horseback shooting at animals with bows. The doors are decorated with two large rings and the heads of gods of Daoism. The doors are decorated with images of phoenix, tigers and dragons. Each side panel is covered with trees, vines, a pagoda, and guardians.

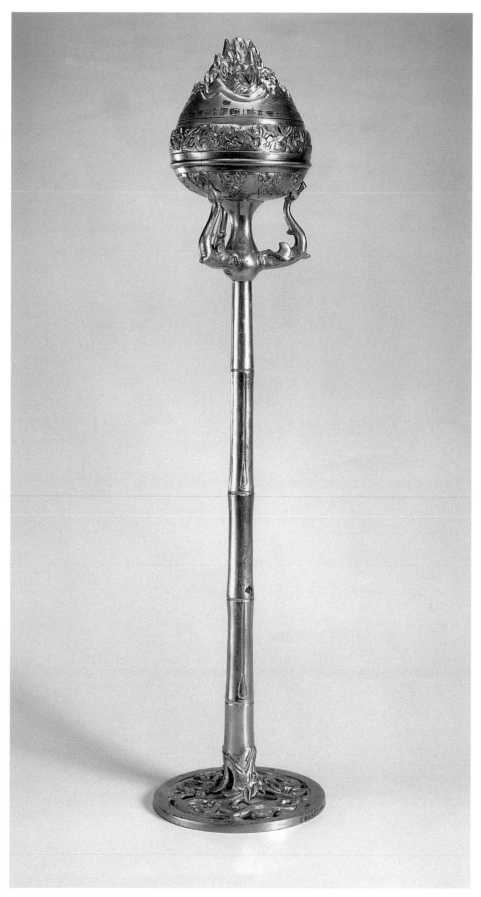

113

Incense Burner or Censer

Bronze with Gold and Silver Gilding; h. 58 cm
Base, d. 13.3 cm
Western Han Dynasty (ca. 137 BC)
Excavated in 1981 from the tomb of Emperor Wu in
Maoling, Xingping County, Shaanxi Province.
Shaanxi History Museum

This gilt bronze incense burner is made up of four parts - the round base containing a dragon at its center, the long bamboo-like stem emanating from the mouth of the dragon, the incense chamber supported by three winged dragons, and the chamber lid in the shape of jagged mountain peaks. The censer was made for the Imperial Palace of Emperor Wu and is thought to have been used by his elder sister, Princess Yangxin. The perforations in the lid allowed the incense to rise like mist from the mountain peaks, creating a powerful illusion of transcending into immortality by way of the rising smoke.

There are two rings of Chinese characters that surround the base and lid of this incense burner. The 35 characters that circle the lid identifies the location of the incense burner within the palace, the date it was made (137 BC), and its weight. The second ring of (33) Chinese characters that can be seen on the base, indicates when it entered the Imperial Palace and shows its registration number in the Imperial catalog.

114
Stone Decorative Tile
Pottery; l. 48 cm, w. 39 cm, d. 6 cm
Eastern Han Dynasty (25-220)
Excavated in Hanzhong Prefecture, Shaanxi Province.
Shaanxi History Museum

This tile bears a relief depicting an official and driver in a carriage. The passenger wears an official robe denoting his position as the master of the tomb. Carriages were popular transport for officials and nobility during the Han dynasty, and often had an umbrella-like canopy decorated with tassels. Tiles such as this were often used to enhance the facade of buildings or tombs.

115
Two Golden Horse Hooves
(1) Gold; h. 3.8 cm, d. 6.5 cm
(2) Gold; h. 3.4 cm, d. 6.5 cm
Western Han Dynasty (206 BC-AD 8)
Excavated in the outskirts of Xianyang, Shaanxi Province.
Shaanxi Xianyang Municipal Museum

These hoof-shaped objects are made of gold. The bases are oval in shape. They were given by the Emperor as a reward for services rendered to the Imperial Court or to the Emperor.

116
Reclining Winged Horse
Pottery; h. 39 cm, l. 55 cm
Western Han Dynasty (206 BC-AD 8)
Excavated in 1991 on the outskirts of Xi'an,
Shaanxi Province.
Shaanxi Xi'an Municipal Relic Protection and
Archaeological Research Center

117
Bell with Winged Horse

Bronze; h. 22.86 cm, w. 14.6 cm
Eastern Han Dynasty (ca. AD 219)
Loan Courtesy of Dr. and Mrs. Bill R. Booth

Bells such as this example were intended to be struck and thus have no clapper. This example is thought to represent the fifth tone in the twelve-tone scale of Chinese music. Decorations include two winged horses. The top is surmounted by two dragons whose bodies curve downward to form a loop from which the bell could hang. Their bodies terminate with their heads sticking out from either side of the top of the bell.

118
Wine Heater

Bronze; h. 11.8 cm, w. 23.8 cm
Western Han Dynasty (206 BC-AD 8)
Excavated in 1981 from pit no. 1 in Maoling, Xingping County, Shaanxi Province.
Shaanxi History Museum

This bronze wine heater consists of three sections: the cup, the stove and the ashtray. The stove is an oval shape sitting on a square base with vertical walls. It has a flat bottom, with four crouching animals for the feet. A handle extends out of the bottom. Under the stove is an oval ashtray, around whose walls are four Gods - the God of the East, White Tiger, Scarlet Bird, and God of the North. On the top of the stove is a container that can be removed.

119

Gilded Bronze Horse

Gilt Bronze; h. 62 cm, l. 82 cm
Western Han Dynasty (206 BC-AD 8)
Excavated in 1981 from an Imperial burial pit at Maoling
in Xingping County, Shaanxi Province.
Shaanxi Maoling Museum

This bronze horse is the only gilded one of its size ever to have been found in China. It was a treasured object used by the Imperial family, possibly during the reign of Emperor Wu. The details of the horse are treated in a naturalistic manner, with the muscles showing some modeling. The mane and tail are finely incised to suggest strands of hair. The tail and genitals were cast separately and soldered onto the cast of the horse prior to gilding. Quality military horses were extremely important to the Han, and in particular to Emperor Wu. This horse might well represent one of the "heavenly horses of Ferghana" which were first brought to China from the West under Wu's orders. Even today, horses from this region (modern Turkmenistan) often demonstrate a golden, almost iridescent coat.

120
Winged Horse
Jade; h. 7 cm, l. 8.9 cm
Western Han Dynasty (206 BC–AD 8)
Excavated in 1966 at Weiling in Xianyang City,
Shaanxi Province.
Shaanxi Xianyang Municipal Museum

This horse and rider are made of white "mutton fat" jade that came from Khotan, in what is now the Xinjiang Autonomous Region. The horse's wings are shown close to the body and its massive legs and the clouds on which its hooves rest make it seem as though it is flying. The rider holds onto the mane with one hand and in the other holds a magic fungus (*lingzhi*) to the horse's neck. In Chinese mythology, horses were thought to be closely related to dragons. Both horses and dragons were endowed with the power of flight, and were capable of transporting their riders to the home of the immortals.

121
Two Cavalry Horses and Riders
Earthenware with Painted Decorations; h. 63 cm, l. 58 cm
Western Han Dynasty (206 BC-AD 8)
Excavated in 1965 from pits near tombs at Yangjiawan,
Xianyang, Shaanxi Province.
Xianyang Museum

The cavalrymen sit with their legs tensed, as if they are prepared to ride off quickly. The horses lack correct anatomical details, but do have painted bridles and girths. The riders sit on saddles, with their legs tightly gripping the horses' shoulders. Prior to the development of the stirrup, this would have been necessary to maintain a secure seat.

122 (opposite page)
Buddha
Jade; h. 38.7 cm, w. 27.8 cm d. 9 cm
Northern Zhou Dynasty (ca. 557-581)
Excavated in 1975 at Lijia Village in Caotan, Xi'an,
Shaanxi Province.
Shaanxi History Museum

The work is rectangular in shape with a niche which shelters the Buddha and two Bodhisattvas who attend the Buddha. Bodhisattvas were followers of Buddha who are reported to have lived perfect lives and as such warranted entry into Nirvana, or a place of enlightenment. The Bodhisattvas chose not to go to Nirvana, but rather to stay behind as guides to the faithful. Buddhism arrived in China over the Silk Roads during the third to sixth centuries AD. It thrived during the Tang dynasty, often receiving the support of the imperial court.

This Buddha sits on a lotus-shaped seat with his hair worn in coils, and wears a kasaya (flowing cassock or Buddhist monk's robe). The sides of the niche are decorated with pearls and lotus flowers. This example of a Buddhist votive stele would have been influenced by Indian examples which could have come to China from Bamiyan (Hindu Kush), and finally by way of the Dunhuang in North-Western China.

123

Painted Female Tomb Figure on Horseback

Glazed Ceramic; h. 37 cm, l. 26.2 cm
Tang Dynasty (ca. AD 664)
Excavated from the tomb of Zheng Rentai in Liquan
County, Shaanxi Province in 1971.
Shaanxi History Museum

The founders of the Tang dynasty originated in northern China where they had close contact with the nomadic horsemen along the border. As such, they brought many of the equestrian traditions, as well as a more liberal approach to the status of women with them to Chang'an. Prior to the Tang, women were not allowed to ride. The dress of this woman rider reflects her northern origins, in particular her black, wide-brimmed hat. Her hair is wrapped in a silk scarf, and she is shown wearing a long white shirt with narrow sleeves over which she has added a red flowered jacket. A long yellow skirt is tied at her waist, and she is wearing a pair of tapered black shoes.

The horse displays a spotted rump calling to mind the modern Appaloosa breed. These spotted horses were extremely popular in China, and examples are seen in several different dynasties. The saddle blanket is delicately embroidered. This figure was found in front of a larger group of figures in the tomb of General Zheng Rentai (601-663) who had served as a brave and famous general. The prominent position of this figure relative to others in the tomb reflects its special status and importance.

This piece is both painted and glazed, and offers an interesting look at pottery techniques just prior to the development of sancai glazes (ca. AD 695) for which the Tang were so famous.

Mirrors are thought to have been made in China since the Eastern Zhou dynasty. They were usually decorated on one side, and highly polished on the other. A silk cord and tassel were attached through a hole in the knob in the center of the decorated side. They were often suspended from belts. Because of their reflective quality, mirrors were often viewed as having magical connotations and as being able to provide protection against evil spirits.

124
Colored Mirror
Bronze; d. 28 cm
Western Han Dynasty (206 BC-AD 8)
Excavated at Hongmiaopo in Xi'an, Shaanxi Province.
Shaanxi History Museum

The handle is on a round base and is painted with vermilion. The painted parts are divided by wave pattern (*huandai*) designs into two sections, an inside ring and an outside ring. The inside ring is composed of four red flowers set against a green background. The outside ring has a vermilion background and portrays three events of *Yeyu* (meeting friends) - dialogue, hunting and hasty travel.

125
Shengxiao Bronze Mirror
Bronze; d. 16.5 cm
Sui Dynasty (589-618)
Excavated on the outskirts of Xian, Shaanxi Province in Shaanxi Province.
Shaanxi History Museum

On the inner ring of the mirror are designs of four gods: the God of the East (the black dragon), the White Tiger, the Scarlet Bird and the God of the North (Xuanhu). The center ring contains the twelve symbols of the Chinese zodiac; the rat, the ox, the tiger, the hare, the snake, the dragon, the horse, the sheep, the monkey, the chicken, the dog and the pig. On the extreme outside ring of the mirror is divided into small triangles.

126
Shouliewen Bronze Mirror
Bronze; d. 14.9 cm
Tang Dynasty (618-907)
Excavated in 1955 in Xi'an, Shaanxi Province.
Shaanxi History Museum

In the center of the decorated side are four hunters on galloping horses each carrying spears bows, arrows, and lassos in their hands. They are chasing deer, hogs, hares and other animals amidst the grass and flowers that decorate the surface.

127

Horse and Rider

Pottery with Sancai (tri-color) glaze; h. 38 cm, l. 52 cm
Tang Dynasty (618-907)
Excavated in 1966 in the western suburbs of Xi'an,
Shaanxi Province.
Shaanxi Xi'an Municipal Relics Protection and
Archaeological Research Center

This horse, with all four legs extended, has an overall glaze of yellow, interspersed with white, blue and green. The rider, who may be either male or female, has deeply set eye sockets and a large nose suggesting that he/she was from an indigenous minority group or a foreign country. The figure carries a traveling bag filled with colored silks behind the saddle. This example of the Tang period is considered a national treasure and while it is often featured in photographs of Tang period horses, it seldom travels outside of China for exhibitions. The horse is extremely beautiful, and the sense of motion and articulation of the muscles makes this a masterpiece of the Chinese pottery.

The epitome of craftsmanship in Tang earthenware sculpture was reserved for the horse. No other subject was as closely studied and skillfully executed. Great care was taken in glazing to emulate the varied coat patterns of specific horses. Actual saddles, tack and decorative features were painstakingly copied by the skilled hands of the potters, all in an effort to satisfy the demands of what William Watson refers to as "the critical eye of a Xi'an [Chang'an] generation of unprecedented horse snobs." The vast majority of Tang horse sculpture depicted the finer horses of the day that invariably showed the size and refinement associated with horses from the West. Also unique to this period was the tendency to present these steeds along with their riders and grooms, in naturalistic, animated poises. Some of the more outstanding examples of Tang horse sculpture were often quite large, measuring around one-half meter or more in height.

128

Tri-Colored Horse

Pottery with Sancai (tri-color) decoration
h. 57 cm, l. 58.7 cm
Tang Dynasty (618-907)
Excavated in 1988 in the western suburbs of Xi'an, Shaanxi Province.
Shaanxi Provincial Archaeological Research Institute

This highly animated yellow-maned horse is complete with a saddle and a highly decorated tack. The bridle, breast strap and crupper are decorated with green flowers and apricot leaves. The horse is stretching his neck and appears to be neighing. The saddle is covered with a blanket where the artist tries to suggest fur by scratching the surface of the clay.

129

Horse With Groom

Glazed Sancai (tri-colored) Pottery;
Man, h. 78.5 cm; Horse, h. 93 cm
Tang Dynasty (618-907)
Excavated in 1995 from the tomb of Prince Li Chongjun in
Fuping County, Shaanxi Province.
Shaanxi Provincial Archaeological Research Institute

130

Horse With Groom

Glazed Sancai (tri-colored) Pottery;
Man, h. 78.5 cm; Horse, h. 93 cm
Tang Dynasty (618-907)
Excavated in 1995 from the tomb of Prince Li Chongjun in
Fuping County, Shaanxi Province.
Shaanxi Provincial Archaeological Research Institute

These two Tang horses and grooms are the largest sancai glazed
sculptures of their type ever discovered. The fact that they were
both from the same tomb, and their similar scale, indicates that
they were probably created as a pair. The grooms' facial features
and dress suggests that they were either foreigners or members of
a minority group. The elaborate decorations shown on the tack of
the white horse signifies that the owner, perhaps Prince Li
Chongjun in whose tomb the two pieces were found, was an
important person who took great pride in the appearance of his
horse.

131

Horse with Saddle

Tri-Colored, Glazed Pottery, h. 72 cm, l. 88 cm
Tang Dynasty (618-907)
Excavated in 1971 from the tomb of Prince Yide in
Qianxian County, Shaanxi Province.
Shaanxi History Museum

132
Twelve Animal (Shengxiao) Figures
Earthenware with Pigment; h. 27-30 cm
Tang Dynasty (618-907)
Excavated in 1950 in the eastern outskirts of Xi'an, Shaanxi Province.
Shaanxi History Museum

These animal figures with human lower torsos represent the Chinese twelve-year cycle in which each year is associated with a particular animal - the rat, ox, tiger, hare, dragon, snake, horse, sheep, monkey, chicken, dog and the pig. A treatise concerning fortune telling written during the Qin dynasty and discovered in 1975 contained the first known listing of the twelve animals of the Chinese zodiac.

133
Polo Players
Terracotta; h. 8.3 cm, l. 13.5 cm
Tang Dynasty (618-907)
Excavated from a Tang dynasty tomb at Guanshan in Lintong County, Shaanxi Province.
Shaanxi History Museum

These terracotta polo players are shown on galloping horses. The riders' bodies are bent as if preparing to strike the ball. Polo is thought to have originated in Persia, and possibly introduced into China by way of Tibet. The game was popular among the nobility during the Tang dynasty.

134 (opposite page)
Girl on a Camel's Back
Earthenware; h. 73 cm, l. 60 cm
Tang Dynasty (618-907)
Excavated in 1986 from a tomb at Hansenzhai, on the eastern suburbs of Xi'an, Shaanxi Province.
Shaanxi Xi'an Municipal Relics Protection and Archaeological Research Center

The young girl sits on the standing camel's back; her head rests on her right arm as if she is sleeping. She wears a long robe and boots. The camel, although slower than the horse, was superior for transporting goods along the Silk Roads.

135

Two "Heavenly King" Tomb Guardians

(1) Earthenware; h. 98 cm
(2) Earthenware; h. 92 cm
Tang Dynasty (618-907)
Excavated in 1972 from a tomb in Xi'an,
Shaanxi Province.
Shaanxi Archaeological Research Institute

These two *tianwang* (heavenly king) funerary objects are stout and ferocious-looking and have highly ornamented costumes which suggests their significance as guardians of the tomb of the Emperor. Their breastplates are covered with gold leaf, and their helmets are decorated with the phoenix, a symbol of the renewal of life. Their sleeves are decorated with animal heads. These warriors have one foot placed upon the head of a monster-like figure underneath them to suggest their supremacy over this creature. Their lively poses are expressions of their gusto and bravery. These figures are artistically exaggerated with their bulging bodies and eyes, and broad mouths and thick necks. All of these characteristics suggest power and the strength of these warriors. They were buried with the dead to protect the Emperor, or nobles from demons, ghosts and grave robbers.

Architectural models of the deceased's home were one of the items commonly placed in tombs. This model has nine houses done in the classical architectural style. There are doors, halls, back chambers and wings for living quarters. On the roofs are glazed tiles. The composition and layout of the courtyard is balanced and symmetrical in conformity with the feudal patriarchal and legal system.

136
Architectural Tomb Model
Earthenware with Sancai (tri-color) decoration; h. 21 cm
Tang Dynasty (618-907)
Excavated at Lingzhao in Chang'an County,
Shaanxi Province.
Shaanxi History Museum

Chinese funerary sculpture produced specifically to be interred within a tomb, first appeared in China during the Shang dynasty. At this time, however, it was much more common to bury actual humans and animals with their masters. The Chinese believed that after their death they would go on to other lives. As such, the buried objects, whether live or sculptural, were intended for their later use. The practice of using sculptural replicas had supplanted the practice of human and animal interment by the Han dynasty. This tradition would continue into the Ming dynasty and is responsible for producing some of China's finest art treasures.

137
Acrobat on Horseback
Pottery; h. 7 cm, l. 12 cm
Tang Dynasty (618-907)
Excavated in Fuping County, Shaanxi Province.
Shaanxi Fupeng County Relics Bureau

This horse, although missing its legs, appears to be in motion. The acrobat is positioned upside-down on its back. Various forms of horse-based entertainment were quite common at the Tang court.

138

Painted Horse with Foreign Groom

Glazed Pottery; Man, h. 60 cm; Horse, h. 80 cm, l. 66 cm
Tang Dynasty (618-907)
Excavated in 1987 at Hansenzhai in Xi'an,
Shaanxi Province.
Shaanxi History Museum

The groom's large nose, beard, large eyes and the belted
robe distinguish this figure as a foreigner. The cosmopolitan nature of early Tang society and the skill of
Central Asians in working with horses often resulted in
their employment as grooms and trainers for the horses
of the nobility.

139
Four Painted Pottery Horses
Earthenware Horses, h. 44-53 cm
Tang Dynasty (618-907)
Excavated in 1966 at pit no. 10, Xi'an, Shaanxi Province.
Shaanxi Provincial Archaeological Research Institute

These are actually four poses of the same horse. All are
unusual in that they have removable saddles, some-
thing not seen in any other examples of Tang sculpture.
Originally, the horses had horsehair manes and tails.
They are one of the most visually vivid and engaging
sets of horses to be found from the Tang dynasty. It was
a common practice for the Tang nobility to raise horses,
not only for use on the battlefields, but also for hunting,
polo and travel.

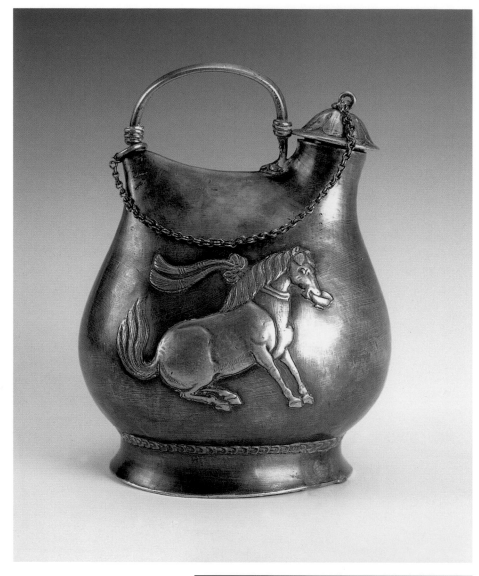

140

Saddle-Flask with Dancing Horse

Silver with Gilt Decoration; h.14.3 cm, d. 2.3 cm;
Base, d. 8.9 cm
Tang Dynasty (618-907)
Excavated in 1970 at Hejia Village in Xi'an,
Shaanxi Province.
Shaanxi History Museum

This flask mimics the shape of the leather bags nomads on northern border of China would attach to their saddles. Large numbers of these flasks, which are usually ceramic (see no. 141), were produced during the Tang, attesting to their popularity.

A gilded horse with a ribbon around its neck and a gold cup in its mouth decorates the center of the flask. This is a reference to the "Dance of the Upturned Cup" performed each year by Emperor Xuanzong's 100 "dancing horses" in honor of his birthday (see page 53). The tradition of performing horses traces back to the Han dynasty, but reached its zenith during the Tang.

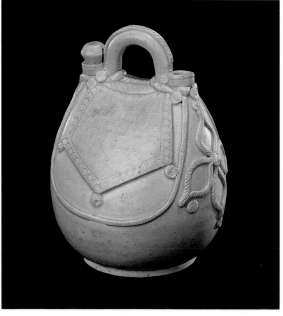

141

White Porcelain Saddle-Flask

Porcelain; h. 20.5 cm, d. 15 cm
Tang Dynasty (618-907)
Excavated at Shapo in Xi'an, Shaanxi Province.
Shaanxi Xi'an Municipal Relics Protection and
Archaeological Research Center

This white glazed porcelain pot has a tiny mouth, and a flared and rounded belly. On the upper body of the flask is a design of a saddle; on the lower portion there are decorative flower petals. Its small spout and shape are reflective of the earlier utilitarian leather wine or water bags indispensable to the nomadic people north and west of China.

142
Civil Official
Painted and Gilded Pottery; h. 69 cm
Tang Dynasty (618-907)
Excavated in 1971 from the tomb of Zheng Rentai in
Liquan County, Shaanxi Province.
Shaanxi History Museum

The figure is dressed in a red robe with loose sleeves,
white trousers and black boots. There are decorative
borders on the cuffs of his sleeves, around his collar,
and along the front of his costume. His headdress is
blue and his breastplate is trimmed in gold. The piece
was possibly modeled after a minister of high rank.

143
Military Officer
Painted and Gilded Pottery; h. 71.5 cm
Tang Dynasty (618-907)
Excavated from a tomb at Zheng Rentai in Liquan County,
Shaanxi Province in 1971.
Shaanxi History Museum

This figure's attitude and costume, decorated with gold
inlay, suggest that he held the high rank of general in
the Imperial army of the Tang Emperor. He originally
held a sword in one hand and a lance in the other. The
figure was cast in Kaolin clay and is white with glazes
applied. This is an example of a masterpiece of unifying
sculpture and painting, which in time would lead to
the three glaze or sancai process associated with the
Tang dynasty.

144

"Dancing" Horse

Glazed Earthenware; h. 49 cm
Tang Dynasty (618-907)
Excavated in 1972 from the tomb of Zhang Shigui in
Liquan County, Shaanxi Province.
Shaanxi Zhaoling Museum

Zhang Shigui (d. 657) was a high ranking military figure under the reign of Emperor Taizong. He was buried near the Imperial mausoleum at Zhaoling. It is thought that this horse represents one of the trained dressage horses taught to dance for the Emperor's enjoyment. Records indicate that dancing horses had been trained since the Han dynasty, with the most famous troupe first performing at the court of Tang Emperor Xuanzong in 729.

Chariot and Horse Decorations

Pottery and Bronze
(1) Dragon-Headed Shaft Decoration, l. 30.4 cm, d. 9.2 cm
(2) Pair Of Stirrups, h. 30 cm, l. 11.3 cm, w. 6.6 cm
(3) Warriors Belt Decoration, h. 10.8 cm, w. 5.5 cm
(4) Horse Decoration, h. 2.5 cm, d. 14 cm
(5) Harness Belt Decoration, Belt End, l. 11.3 cm, w. 5 cm;
*   Belt Loop, h. 2.8 cm, l. 6.3 cm, w. 2 cm*
(6) Chariot Ornaments, h. 9 cm
(7) Pottery Jar, h. 37 cm, d. 23 cm
Tang Dynasty (618-907)
Excavated in 1997 from a tomb in Xinzhu Town of Xian,
Shaanxi Province.
Shaanxi History Museum

The group of items (1) through (6) was found in the pottery jar, item (7). As bronze was quite valuable at the time, it is thought that these items were buried for protection.

(1) This piece would have decorated the end of a carriage pole and was originally gilded.

(2) Stirrups, essential for securing a stable seat on the back of a horse, were first invented in China circa 322. By the Tang, different styles of stirrups were used to differentiate the rank, age or sex of the rider.

(3) The warrior's belt decoration shows a warrior wearing a helmet, armor, and high boots

(4) This circular shaped decoration was used for a chariot ornament; its borders are covered with flower petals.

(5) This harness part consists of the buckle, or head, and the keeper through which the leather belt would have passed.

(6) These bronze chariot ornaments are hollow and have a flower shaped head.

(7) The pottery jar in which all of these six different, but related, items were found is a simple clay pot, but one which held a wealth of treasure, both artistically and historically.

Horse Bit

Iron; l. 22 cm
Tang Dynasty (618-907)
Excavated in 1972 at Bianjiazhuang in Longxian County,
Shaanxi Province.
Shaanxi Longixian County Museum

This type of bit (*xian*) is somewhat similar to a modern jointed Pelham type. It is thought that this type of bit was used in Asia from the sixth century.

147
Tri-Colored Phoenix Ewer
Glazed Sancai Pottery; h. 34 cm, d. 13.5 cm
Tang Dynasty (618-907)
Excavated in 1959 at Linjia Village in Sanqiao, Xi'an,
Shaanxi Province.
Shaanxi Xi'an Municipal Relics Protection and
Archaeological Research Center

This ewer has a small mouth, narrow neck, and a single
handle. Its design reflects influences from Central Asia.
There are decorative designs on both sides of the pot - a
phoenix on one side and a hunter on horseback on the
other.

148
Tri-Colored Female Court Figure
Glazed Pottery; h. 44.5 cm
Tang Dynasty (618-907)
Excavated in l959 from a tomb at Zhongbao Village in the western suburbs of Xi'an.
Shaanxi History Museum

This is an extraordinary example of a woman of the Tang court. The figure wears a long sleeved blue blouse with yellow designs, a yellow skirt and pointed shoes. She is plump, and has soft eyes and a small, red-lipped mouth. It is interesting to note that Emperor Ming Huang's (685-762) favorite concubine, Yang Kuei-fei, was somewhat overweight. It therefore became the fashion to imitate her appearance. This piece, with her moon-shaped face, pale skin, loose fitting garments, represents a style that was briefly in vogue during the Tang dynasty.

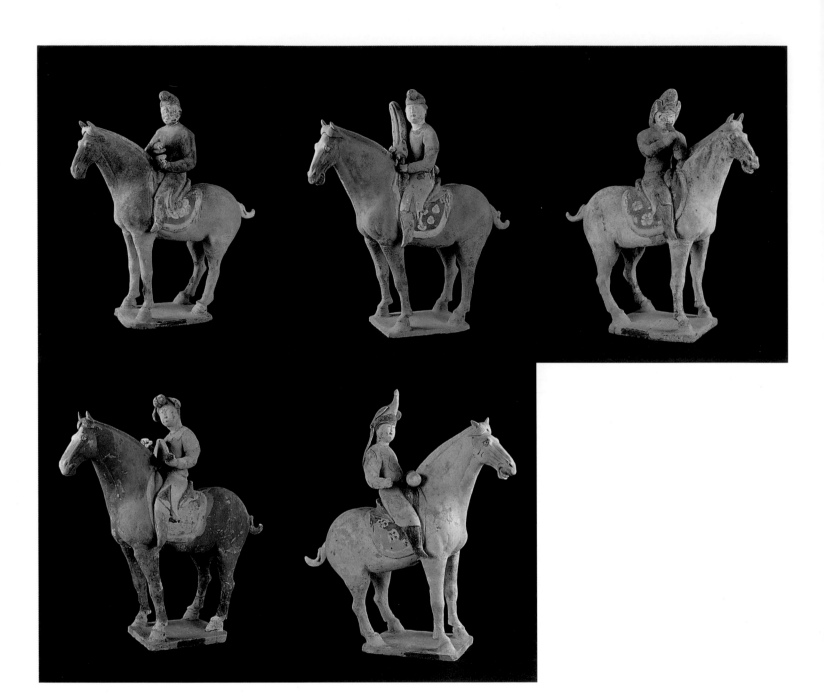

149

Women Musicians on Horseback

Set of five pieces
Glazed Pottery; h. 33-37 cm, l. 34-35 cm
Tang Dynasty (618-907)
Excavated in Huokou on the eastern outskirts of Xi'an, Shaanxi Province.
Shaanxi Xi'an Municipal Relics Collection and Archaeological Research Center

Each of the five musicians wears a cap, tight-sleeved robe and pointed shoes which are placed in the stirrups. Their dress and musical instruments - the *xiao* (a vertical bamboo flute), cymbals, *konghou* (a stringed instrument which is plucked), and drums - reflect the popularity of music from the West that first arrived in China during the Han and continued through the Tang dynasties. Troupes of female musicians often provided entertainment at the elaborate outings enjoyed by the rich of Chang'an.

150

Mounted Hunters

Set of five pieces
Glazed Pottery; h. 33-38 cm, l. 34 cm
Tang Dynasty (618-907)
Excavated from the tomb of a county magistrate at Jinxiang in the eastern suburbs of Xi'an, Shaanxi Province.
Shaanxi Xi'an Municipal Relics Protections and Archaeological Research Center

This grouping depicts a hunting party of two Chinese women and three men. The deep eye sockets, large noses, protruding cheeks and facial hair shown on all of the men would indicate that they are foreigners, probably from Central Asia. During the early Tang dynasty, women enjoyed much more freedom than in previous or subsequent dynasties. They pursued active lifestyles including hunting and polo. Four of the five figures are accompanied by hunting animals including a falcon, small dog, a linx, and what is probably a cheetah. Cheetahs were not native but were often imported to Tang China along with their foreign trainers. The fifth hunter, one of the women, is shown with a deer carcass across the rump of her horse.

This series of photos depicts the paintings discovered on the walls of the entry hall of the tomb of Tang Prince Li Xian. They are extremely fragile, and are of such artistic and cultural significance that any exposure to travel, strong light, or changing humidity could cause irreparable damage. As such, the original paintings are never placed on public exhibition.

The original of this tomb mural is 100-200 cm high and 980 cm long. It was divided into several parts when it was removed. Specialists pasted strong cloth to the front of the original murals and essentially peeled them off the walls. The original surfaces would have been made of mud that was strengthened with hemp fibers. The murals were later framed and moved into secure vaults in the Shaanxi History Museum where the light and humidity are strictly controlled.

151

Polo Match Tomb Painting
(Reproduction)
Paint Over Mud Mixed with Hemp Fibers;
h. 196 cm, w. 154 cm
Tang Dynasty (618-907)
Excavated in 1971 from the entrance of the Tomb of Prince Li Xian in Qianxian County, Shaanxi Province.
Shaanxi History Museum

Polo originated in Persia and was brought to China during the Tang dynasty. It became a popular diversion at the royal court, with even emperors sometimes participating in the games. The players in this painting control their horses with their left hands and hold their mallets in their right hands. It provides important artistic evidence of ancient Chinese sport, and documents the cultural and social interaction of China and western Asia during the period.

152

Hunting Scene 1
(Reproduction)
Paint over Mud Mixed with Hemp;
(1) h. 149.5 cm, w. 185.5 cm
Tang Dynasty (618-907)
Original excavated in 1971 from the Tomb of Prince Li Xian in Qianxian County, Shaanxi Province.
Shaanxi History Museum

The Prince, Li Xian, is shown on the white horse and is escorted by over forty hunters on horseback with bows and arrows. Two camels that carry provisions for the hunt follow the hunting party. There is a great sense of movement, and the swirling flags of the Prince's attendants demonstrate his importance.

153

Hunting Scene 2

(Reproduction)

Paint over Mud Mixed with Hemp;
(2) h. 174 cm, w. 220 cm
Tang Dynasty (618-907)
Original excavated in 1971 from the Tomb of Prince Li
Xian in Qianxian County, Shaanxi Province.
Shaanxi History Museum

154

Hunting Scene 3

(Reproduction)

Paint over Mud Mixed with Hemp;
(3) h. 209 cm, w. 60.5 cm
Tang Dynasty (618-907)
Original excavated in 1971 from the Tomb of Prince Li
Xian in Qianxian County, Shaanxi Province.
Shaanxi History Museum

155
Painted Saddle Horse
Painted Pottery; h. 27.8 cm, l. 31 cm
Yuan Dynasty (1279-1368)
Excavated from a Yuan tomb at Weiqu in Chang'an
County, Shaanxi Province.
Shaanxi History Museum

The horse is painted white with its mane pulled to one side. It has a large, oval saddle skirt typical of the Yuan dynasty and its Mongol founders. It is also interesting to note the diminutive size of the Mongolian-type horse opposed to the larger and more refined horses depicted in Tang sculpture. The Tang horses represented the best of China's equines, and owed their superior size and refinement to imports from Central Asia. Even during the Tang, the average horse would probably closely resemble the Yuan example shown here.

156
Horse with Rider
Painted Pottery; h. 42 cm, l. 39 cm
Yuan Dynasty (1279-1368)
Excavated from a Yuan tomb at Weiqu in Chang'an
County, Shaanxi Province.
Shaanxi History Museum

The rider is made of gray pottery and he wears a helmet, a robe and leather boots. He carries a quiver for arrows on his back, and is most likely a cavalryman. The horse's tack is beautifully detailed. The saddle has tooled leather skirts and is secured with a crupper that fits snugly under the horse's tail, and a breast strap in front. During this period it was customary to wrap the horse's tail.

157
Gray Pottery Carriage
Pottery; h. 31 cm, l. 42.5 cm
Yuan Dynasty (1279-1368)
Excavated on the outskirts of Xi'an, Shaanxi Province.
Shaanxi Provincial Archaeological Research Institute

This model of a carriage from the Yuan dynasty is typical of the transportation available to the wealthy people of the time. The ends of the shaft are shaped like dragons. Each of the two wheels has sixteen spokes, and there are bars on the two windows on either side of the carriage. The roof is a type common to nomadic tribesmen.

Imperial processions were elaborate affairs, strictly governed by rules and traditions. These were often reproduced in miniature and are suggestive of a much larger number of people, who would have accompanied the Emperor or a member of the royal family whenever they traveled. The number of figures that are seen in such sets often number in the hundreds and include maidens, musicians, guards of honor, troupes of officials and carts, chariots, carriages and men on horseback.

158

Mounted Honor Guard

A set of twelve pieces
Glazed Pottery; h. 32.5-39 cm
Ming Dynasty (1368-1644)
Excavated at Jianwangjing in Chang'an County,
Shaanxi Province.
Shaanxi History Museum

These riders are part of an Imperial procession. They wear tight-sleeved robes with belts over which they have red or green tunics that symbolized their rank. They are playing musical instruments. Their horses have breast straps and have harness decorations on their faces. These musicians would have been in the vanguard of the guard of honor for the Emperor. He would have ridden behind them in a covered carriage.

159

Men of the Honor Guard

A set of eleven pieces
Glazed Ceramic; h. 20.5 - 24 cm
Ming Dynasty (1368-1644)
Excavated from a tomb at Jianwangjing in Chang'an
County, Shaanxi Province.
Shaanxi History Museum

These figures, like those in the mounted honor guard, were a part of an Imperial procession. They wear various colored robes, hats and represent different levels of officials who would have served the Emperor in some capacity. Their costumes are red, white or green, with cross flaps or rounded collars. Others in the party have various headdresses or hairstyles.

160

Women Guard of Honor

A set of seven pieces
Glazed Pottery; h. 21-23 cm
Ming Dynasty (1368-1644)
Excavated at Jianwangjing in Chang'an County, Shaanxi
Province.
Shaanxi History Museum

These women would have been a part of a much larger
contingent of honor guards participating in the
Emperor's procession.

161
Hunting Scene, Scroll Painting
Watercolor on Paper; h. 28.2 cm, l. 271.5 cm
Qing Dynasty (1644-1911)
Shaanxi History Museum

There are altogether thirty-three horses and riders in this composition. On the left there is a group of hunters killing a tiger. On the right, other hunters are hurrying to join in the battle. The painting is representative of the style of the Qing dynasty.

162
Gilded Stirrups
Gilt on Iron; h. 18 cm, l. 15.5 cm, w. 12.5 cm
Qing Dynasty (1644-1911)
Excavated on the outskirts of Xian, Shaanxi Province.
Shaanxi History Museum

The treads of the stirrups are oval in shape. The sides feature two dragons playing with a ball. At the top of the stirrups are rectangular holes for fastened the stirrups to the saddle. The beards of the dragons curl backward and their backs are decorated with a *mancao* (entwined vines pattern) design. Holes in the treads allow water to drain. The dragons are embellished with gold.

163
Horse Hitching Post
Stone; h. 163 cm
Qing Dynasty (1644-1911)
Shaanxi Xi'an Beilin Museum

Stone hitching posts were quite common in China during the Qing dynasty. This example shows a man riding a lion. Holes created by this design provided riders with a convenient place to tie their reins.

164

Saddle with Bridle and Stirrups

Saddle: Wood, Leather with Cloisonné, h. 30-22.5 cm, l. 55 cm.
Stirrups: Iron with Silver Inlay
Qing Dynasty (ca. Late 17th or Early 18th Century)
Thought to have been made in Beijing
From the Collection of the International
Museum of the Horse

The complete saddle was originally purchased from a descendant of a Mongolian noble family who stated that it was presented to their ancestor by the Qing Emperor for meritorious military service. To protect the saddle from destruction by the Red Guard during the Cultural Revolution, the saddle was painted red. Traces of this paint are still visible on the underside of the saddletree.

Bibliography

Banks, Barbara Chapman. "The Magical Powers of the Horse as Revealed in the Archeological Explorations of Early China." Ph.D. diss., University of Chicago, 1989.

Bland, J. O. P. *Recent Events and Present Policies in China*. London: J. P. Lippincott Company, 1912.

Blunden, Caroline and Mark Elvin. *The Cultural Arts of the World: China*. Alexandria, Va.: Stonehenge Press, 1991.

Bower, Virginia L. "Polo in Tang China: Sport and Art." *Asian Art* (winter 1991): 22-45.

Booth, B. R. *Masterpieces from the National Palace Museum*. Taipei, Taiwan: National Palace Museum, The Republic of China, 1983.

Booth, B. R. "Oriental Motifs in 19th Century European and American Art." *Bulletin of The National Museum of History* no. 12 (December 1981) Published by the National Museum of History, Taipei, Taiwan, The Republic of China.

Brown, J. Carter. *The Exhibition of Archaeological Finds of the People's Republic of China*. Washington, D. C.: National Gallery of Art, 1974.

Chafee, John W. *The Thorny Gates of Learning in Sung China*. Cambridge: Cambridge University Press, 1985.

Chen Quanfan, et al. *Xi'an: Legacies of Ancient Chinese Civilization*. Beijing: Morning Glory Press, 1992.

Cheung Dan, Diane, ed. *Terra-cotta Warriors and Horses of Emperor Qin Shi Huang*. Hong Kong: Man Hai Language Publications, 1988.

China Pictoral Publications, ed. *Vistas of China*. Beijing: China Pictorial Publishing Co., 1987.

Clunas, Craig. *Art in China*. Oxford: Oxford University Press. 1997.

Coates, Austin. *China Races*. Oxford: Oxford University Press, 1994.

Coyle, M. J., J. Livingston and J. Highland, eds. *China Yesterday and Today*. New York: Bantam Books, 1984.

Cutton-Brock, Juliet. *Horse Power: A History of the Horse and the Donkey in Human Society*. Cambridge, Mass.: Harvard University Press, 1992.

Creel, H.G. "The Role of the Horse in Chinese History." *American Historical Review* 70, no. 3 (April 1965): 647-672.

Crossley, Pamela Kyle. *The Manchus*. Cambridge, Mass.: Blackwell Publishers, 1997.

Curtin, Jeremiah. *The Mongols: A History*. Conshohocken, Penn.: Combined Books, 1996. Originally published Boston: Little Brown and Co., 1908.

d'Argence, Rene-Yvon Lefebvre. *Ancient Chinese Bronzes in the Avery Brundage Collection*. Berkley: Diablo Press, 1966.

Dien, Albert E. "The Stirrup and Its Effect on Chinese Military History," *Ars Orientalis* 16 (1986): 33-56.

Ebrey, Patricia Buckley, ed. *Chinese Civilization: A Sourcebook*. New York: Free Press, 1981.

Epstein, H. *Domestic Animals of China*. US edition. New York: Africana Publishing Corp., 1971.

Fairbanks, John K. *China: The People's Middle Kingdom and the U.S.A*. Cambridge, Mass.: Belknap Press of Harvard University Press, 1967.

_____. *The Great Chinese Revolution: 1800-1985*. New York: Harper & Row, 1987.

_____ and Merle Goldman. *China: A New History*. Cambridge: Cambridge, Mass.: Belknap Press of Harvard University Press, 1992.

Fitzgerald, C. P., ed. *The Horizon History of China*. New York: American Publishing Co., 1969.

Frazer, John. *The Chinese: Portrait of a People*. New York: Summit Books, 1944.

Froneck, Thomas, ed. *Arts of China*. New York: American Heritage Publishing Co., 1969.

Frye, Richard N. *The Heritage of Central Asia From Antiquity to the Turkish Expansion*. Princeton, New Jersey: Markus Wiener Publishers, 1998.

Gernet, Jacques. *Daily Life in China on the Eve of the Mongol Invasion 1250-1276*. Trans. H. M Wright. Stanford: Stanford University Press, 1962.

_____. *A History of Chinese Civilization*. 2d ed. Cambridge, England: Cambridge University Press, 1996. Reprint 1999.

Goodrich, Chauncey S. "Riding Astride and the Saddle in Ancient China." *Harvard Journal of Asiatic Studies* 44, no. 2 (December 1984): 279-306.

Harrist, Robert E, Jr. *Power and Virtue: The Horse in Chinese Art*. New York: China Institute in America, 1997.

Hendricks, Bonnie L. *International Encyclopedia of Horse Breeds*. Norman, Okla.: University of Oklahoma Press, 1995.

Hildinger, Erik. *Warriors of the Steppe: A Military History of Central Asia, 500 BC to 1700 AD*. New York: Sarpedon, 1997.Hong, Yang. Weapons of Ancient China. Beijing: Science Press, 1992.

Hopkirk, Peter. *Foreign Devils on the Silk Road*. Amherst, Mass.: University of Massachusetts Press, 1980.

Hucker, Charles O. *China's Imperial Past: An Introduction to Chinese History and Culture*. Stanford: Sanford University Press, 1975.

Hyland, Ann. *The Medieval Warhorse: From Byzantium to the Crusades*. London: Grange Books, 1994.

Jagchid, Sechin, and Van Jay Symons. *Peace, War, and Trade Along the Great Wall*. Indianapolis: Indiana University Press, 1989.

Keightley, D. N. "The Religious Commitment: Shang Theology and the Genesis of Political Culture." *History of Religion* 17, nos. 3-4 (1977-78).

Kroll, Paul W. "The Dancing Horses of T'ang." T'oung Pao LXVII, no. 3-5 (1981): 240-269.

Lau, Aileen, ed. *Spirit of Han*. Singapore: Southeast Asian Ceramic Society, 1991; Singapore: Sun Tree Limited, 1998.

Lau, D. C., and Roger T. Ames. *Sun Pin: The Art of Warfare*. New York: Ballantine Books, 1996.

Lawton, Thomas. *New Perspectives on Chu Culture During the Eastern Zhou Period*. Princeton, New Jersey: Arthur M. Sackler Gallery, Smithsonian Institute in association with Princeton University Press, 1991.

Lee, Sherman E. *A History of Far Eastern Art*. Englewood, New Jersey: Prentice-Hall, 1982.

Lei Congyun, Yang Yang and Zhao Gushan. *Imperial Tombs of China*. Trans. Richard E. Strassberg and Martha Avery. Memphis, Tenn.: Lithograph Publishing, 1995.

Li Jian, ed. *Eternal China: Splendors from the First Dynasties*. Dayton, Ohio: Dayton Art Institute, 1998.

Loewe, Michael. *Everyday Life in Early Imperial China: During the Han Period 202 BC - AD 220*. New York: Dorset Press, 1968.

Maslow, Jonathan. "The Golden Horse of Turkmenistan." *Aramco World* 48, no. 5 (May/June 1997). 15 November 1999 http://www.silk-road.com/.

Michaelson, Carol. *Gilded Dragon: Buried Treasures from China's Golden Ages*. London: British Museum Press, 1999.

Narahiro, Toshio, Eun Hyun Yum and Taskeshi Kuno. *Great Sculpture of the Far East*. New York: Reynal & Co., 1979.

Needham, Joseph. *Science and Civilisation in China*. vol. 4, *Physics and Physical Technology, part 2: Mechanical Engineering*. Cambridge, England: Cambridge University Press, 1965.

Olsen, Sandra, ed. *Horses Through Time*. Boulder, Colo.: Roberts Rinehart Publishers for Carnegie Museum of Natural History, no date.

Paludan, Ann. *Chronicle of the Chinese Emperors*. London: Thames and Hudson. 1998.

Piggott, Stuart. *The Earliest Wheeled Transport From the Atlantic Coast to the Caspian Sea*. London: Thames and Hudson, 1983.

"Polo." Silk Road Foundation. 1997. 15 November 1999 <http://www.silk-road.com/games.shtml.>

Rawson, Jessica. *Ancient China: Art and Archaeology*. New York: Harper & Row, 1980.

Reichwein, Adolph. *China and Europe: Intellectual and Artistic Contacts in the Eighteenth Century*. Trans. J. C. Powell. London: Kegan Paul, Trench, Trubner & Co., 1925.

Rogers, Howard, ed. *China 5,000 Years: Innovation and Transformation in the Arts*. New York: Harry N. Abrams for Guggenheim Museum Publications, 1998.

Rossabi, Morris. *Kubilai Khan: His Life and Times*. Berkley: University of California Press, 1988.

Sawyer, Ralph D. trans. *The Art of the Warrior: Leadership and Strategy from the Chinese Military Classics*. Boston: Shambhala Publications, 1996.

Seybolt, Peter. *Throwing the Emperor from His Horse: Portrait of a Village Leader in China, 1923-1995*. Boulder, Colo.: Westview Press, 1996.

Shaughnessy, Edward L. *Sources of Western Zhou History: Inscribed Bronze Vessels*. Berkley: University of California Press, 1991.

So, Jenny F., and Emma C. Bunker. *Traders and Raiders on China's Northern Frontier*. Seattle: Arthur M. Sackler Gallery, Smithsonian Institute in association with the University of Washington Press, 1995.

Spence, Jonathan D. *Emperor of China: Self Portrait of K'ang-hsi*. Reissue ed. New York: Vintage Books, 1988.

Spruytte, J. *Early Harness Systems: Experimental Studies*. Trans. Mary Littauer. London: J. A. Allen, 1983.

Sun Ji. "The Equestrian Gear and Ornament of the Tang Dynasty." *Wenwu* 10 (1981): 82-88, 96.

_____. Personal interview. Beijing, 17 March 1999.

Sun Tzu. *The Illustrated Art of War*. Trans. Thomas Cleary. Boston: Shambhala Publications, 1998.

Sullivan, Michael. *The Arts of China*. 3rd ed. Berkley: University of California Press, 1984.

Temple, Robert. *The Genius of China: 3,000 Years of Science, Discovery, and Invention*. United Kingdom: Multimedia Publications, 1986.

Thorp, Robert L. *Son of Heaven: Imperial Arts of China*. Seattle: Son of Heaven Press, 1988.

Waley, Arthur. "The Heavenly Horse of Ferghana: A New View." *History Today* (February 1955): 95-103.

_____. *Translations from the Chinese*. New York: Alfred A. Knopf, 1941.

Watt, C. Y. and Anne E. Woodwell. *When Silk was Gold: Central Asia and Chinese Textiles*. New York: Harry N. Abrams for Metropolitan Museum of Art, 1997.

Wenley, A. G. *Ming Porcelains in the Freer Gallery of Art*. Washington, D. C.: Smithsonian Institute, 1953.

Wong, Grace and Goh Ngee Hui. *The Silk Road: Treasures of Tang China*. Singapore: Historical and Cultural Exhibitions PTE, The Empress Press, 1991.

Wriggins, Sally Hovey. *Xuanzang: A Buddhist Pilgrim on the Silk Road*. Boulder, Colo.: Westview Press, 1996.

Wu Yong-qi and Cheng Yue Hua, eds. *Bronze Chariots and Horses at Qin Mausoleum*. Hong Kong: Tai Dai Publishing, 1989.

Wu Zilin, *Terra-cotta Figures and Bronze Horse at Qin Mausoleum*. Xi'an, P. R. C.: Qin Shi Huang Mausoleum Museum, 1986.

Wu Zilin and Gaua Xingwen. *Qin Shi Huang, The First Emperor of China*. Hong Kong: Man Hai Language Publications, 1988.

Xiao Shiling. *China's Cultural Heritage: Rediscovering a Past 7,000 Years*. Beijing: Morning Glory Publishers, 1995.

Xiaoneng Yang, ed. *The Golden Age of Chinese Archaeology: Celebrated Discoveries from the People's Republic of China*. New Haven: Yale University Press for the National Gallery of Art, Washington, DC, 1999.

Yu Weichao, ed. *A Journey into China's Antiquity*. vol. 3. Beijing: Morning Glory Press for National Museum of Chinese History, 1997.

Zou Zongxu. *The Land Within the Passes: A History of Xian*. Trans. Susan Whitfield. New York: The Viking Press, 1991. Originally published as Qian Nian Gu Du Xi An (Hong Kong: Commercial Press, 1987)

Index

H

Harness: 26, 29, 31, 33, 47
    Throat-and-Girth: 33-34
    Breast-Strap: 35
    Collar: 36
    artifacts: 76,79,82,92, 103, 104, 106-
        110, 116, 164, 165
H. G. Creel: 44
Han Dynasty: 27, 28, 33, 35, 36, 37, 41,
        43, 44, 45, 46, 47, 48, 50,
        51, 54, 55, 58,
    artifacts: 128-140
Hangzhou: 59
Haojing: 40
Heavenly Horses
    War of the Heavenly Horses: 42
    mythical horses and dragons: 54
    artifacts: 136, 137
Hebei: 50, 61
Horse armor: 39-40
Horseback Riding in China: 31-34
Hu: 30
Hun: 37
huozhu: 51

I

Iran: 29

J

jia qi ju zhuang: 39
jiadai: 50
Jiangsu: 48
Jiangxia: 55
Jin Dynasty: 39, 51
jin'gen-che: 40
jisheng: 51
Jundushan: 36
Jurchen invasion: 57

K

Kaifeng: 56
Kangxi: 61
Khitan: 59, 61
Khotan: 48
Khubilai Khan: 28, 59, 60

Khuttal: 48
King Cambyses: 39
King Wu Ling: 37
King Wuding: 30
Kirghiz: 48
Kish: 48
Kokand: 48
kuai ti: 44

L

Lefebvre des Noëttes: 34
Li Guangli: 42, 43
Li He: 40
Li Si: 44
Liang: 54
Liao Dong: 40
li-che: 32, 40
Linzi: 55
Liu Wei: 40
Liu Xu: 49
Li Yong: 55
lu-che: 40
luotou: 49

M

Ma Shi Huang: 55
Maimargh: 48
Manchu: 27, 28, 61, 62
Marco Polo: 59
mian lian: 39
Ming Dynasty: 28, 60, 61, 150, 165
    artifacts: 165-167
Mo Di: 35
Mo Tzu: 35
Mongol: 27, 28, 29, 44, 48, 56, 57, 58,
        59, 60, 61
    Mongol invasion: 57-58

N

Nanjing: 39, 52, 60
Nestorian: 46
nian-che: 40
Nisean: 48

X

xian: 50
Xianyang: 32, 50, 51
xiao-rong: 40
xingye: 50, 51
Xiongnu: 27, 33, 37, 41, 42, 44, 45, 46
Xuanzong: 49, 52, 54, 55, 56
Xunzi: 30

Y

yandai: 50
Yangjiawan: 42, 51
Yili River: 44, 48
Yongle: 60
youle: 50
Yuan Dynasty: 27, 28, 51, 56, 57, 59, 60
    artifacts: 164
yunzhu: 51

Z

zhang ni: 50
Zhang Qian: 41, 42, 44
Zhang Yuo: 52, 53, 54
Zhanguoce: 41
Zhao: 37
Zhao Ling: 50
Zhao Zu: 41
Zheng He: 60
Zhou Dynasty: 27, 30, 31, 32, 33, 35,
                36, 40, 50, 56, 65
    artifacts: 74-119
Zhu Yuanzhang: 60